'An earnest, affectionate trawl through the archives with comments from some of the thousands whose lives Peel touched' *Sunday Times*

'A leisurely stroll through the life of an "irreplaceable man" . . . providing thoughtful, well-paced portraits of the national treasure du jour . . . [They] recreate the sense of personality that Peel always conveyed . . . to create two warm tributes to a much-missed DJ' *Observer*

'If you don't know much about the fella, ask your dad, or simply read this lightly written biography . . . Perfect for dads!' *OK*

'In Mick Wall we have an author who knows his onions . . . He's bashed out nearly 200 pages here and got his hands on some great pictures - light on sex and drugs but heavy, man, on the rock'n'roll' *Ireland on Sunday*

Mick Wall was the founding editor of *Classic Rock* magazine and currently writes for *Mojo*. He first met John Peel in the late seventies, when he worked for *Sounds* magazine, where the Peel column was then a weekly highlight. Wall is also the author of several music books, including titles on Guns N' Roses, Don Arden and Ozzy Osbourne. He ghosted the recent bestselling Status Quo autobiography, *XS All Areas*, and is a former presenter for Sky TV and Capital Radio. In the late eighties he was a regular guest on Andy Kershaw's Sunday afternoon Radio 1 show, through which he became reacquainted, for a time, with Peel. Although Mick met John on only a few occasions, like all the millions of fans who followed the Peel show over the years, he felt he enjoyed an intimate bond with the great man through his extraordinary work on the radio. Peel also once showed him how to use the coffee machine at the BBC, for which the author remains eternally grateful.

By Mick Wall

Diary of a Madman:
the Authorised Biography of Ozzy Osbourne
Guns N' Roses: The Most Dangerous Band in the World
Pearl Jam
Paranoid: Black Days with Sabbath & Other Horror Stories
Mr Big: Ozzy, Sharon and My Life as the Godfather of Rock
(Don Arden with Mick Wall)
XS All Areas: the Autobiography of Status Quo
(with Mick Wall)
John Peel: A tribute to the much-loved DJ and broadcaster

JOHN PEEL

*A tribute to the much-loved
DJ and broadcaster*

Mick Wall

ORION

An Orion paperback

First published in Great Britain in 2004
by Orion
This paperback edition published in 2005
by Orion Books Ltd,
Orion House, 5 Upper St Martin's Lane,
London WC2H 9EA

1 3 5 7 9 10 8 6 4 2

A CIP catalogue record for this book is available
from the British Library.

ISBN 0 75287 674 0

Printed and bound in Great Britain by Clays Ltd, St Ives plc

www.orionbooks.co.uk

CONTENTS

PREFACE

As a Radio 1 DJ, John Peel will be remembered for many things – not least his laconic, understated style of presentation, his droll, bone-dry sense of humour, and his surprisingly erudite, almost poetic use of the English language. He was one of those rare DJs for whom you turned the volume higher for what he had to say than you sometimes did for what he actually played. That said, he will also be remembered as the man who single-handedly discovered and, most crucially, played first on British radio almost all of the most important singers and musicians of the past forty years. And yet, for all his listeners, whatever our entry point – from Country Joe & the Fish to PJ Harvey, via T. Rex and the Smiths – it was, in retrospect, not so much the rare and unusual artists he introduced us to that ultimately fascinated us about his shows, as our discovery of Peel himself, and the unique relationship he engaged in with his audience.

Unlike almost every other DJ until he came along, who tended to shout at their audience, Peel addressed his listeners as though he were actually in the room talking to you alone. Famous for playing records at the wrong speed, mumbling incomprehensibly about a family member, being caught out by the sudden end of a track, and playing records that were only available from a shop in Cairo that only opened on a Thursday – none of that mattered once he opened his radio mic and started speaking to you like a best friend. Which is exactly what he became to those of us who fell under his spell over the years: a close and trusted friend, who would never knowingly lie to you or steer you down the wrong path. Modest about his own achievements, he once described his career with typical understatement: 'You can either see it as selfless dedication to public-service broadcasting, or a shocking lack of ambition.' In fact, he added, 'It's both of those things. I never make stupid mistakes. Only very, very clever ones ...'

I was fourteen when I 'discovered' John Peel. It was 1972 and I was absolutely besotted with Rod Stewart and the Faces. Any magazine or newspaper that carried a story about them, or even just a picture, I would buy immediately. After I'd finished absorbing every single word and read it at least twice, the story would be cut out with scissors and glued into the scrapbook; the pictures would go straight onto my bedroom wall. The same with any TV or radio programme that they appeared on – I would be ready with the microphone in my hand, waiting to tape it on the little Philips cassette player with the chunky keyboard buttons my mum had bought me for Christmas. (Video? What was that? I was still trying to persuade my parents to invest in one of the new colour tellies that had just become available.)

In this way, I discovered a great many TV and radio programmes in the early seventies that, despite how the history books tend to depict that pre-MTV age now, did actually play some decent music from time to time. There was *Top of the Pops*, of course, which Rod and the Faces did when they had singles out; and as this was still the era when 'serious' album-oriented artists generally only released one single per album, that meant they might be on, in all, maybe half a dozen times a year, often less.

Fortunately, however, there was also, as I discovered late one night, something called *The Old Grey Whistle Test*, an album-oriented TV show on BBC2 presented by someone called Bob Harris, this studious, older-brother-type guy with one of those beards that obscured his mouth and made him perpetually look as if he was mumbling. The Faces had been billed as performing live on the show that night and I had been able to obtain special dispensation from my parents to stay up late so that I could be there to commit this momentous occurrence to tape. After that first occasion, bored though I often was by the procession of leaden singer-songwriters that characterised most editions of *The Old Grey Whistle Test* in the early seventies, I began to discover little diamonds in the dirt like David Bowie,

Roxy Music, Queen, Pink Floyd, Genesis, Yes, Little Feat and countless others, all of whom I saw play live – and taped – for the first time on *The Old Grey Whistle Test*.

There were other TV shows that featured singers and groups performing, or more usually miming, to their singles – *Lift Off With Ayshea*, *Supersonic*, *Saturday Morning Swap Shop*, and all the usual little guest spots where someone like Bowie, Elton or Stewart might crop up – the *Russell Harty Show*, the *Lulu Show* and so on. But for the good stuff – the non-singles stuff – apart from *The Old Grey Whistle Test*, the only other programme that I remember regularly taping back then was the BBC2 *In Concert* series. Once again, I only came across it by chance after my dad told me he'd read in the paper that Rod Stewart was going to be on the telly that night. As I recall, the concert was also broadcast live simultaneously on Radio 1, and I viewed the occasion as a major microphonic event.

Curiously, considering I now possess almost nothing else from those days, I still have a recording of that programme. It was presented by a Radio 1 DJ I had never heard of before: John Peel. I recall mistaking him at first for someone from the audience who had just wandered onto the stage to say something to the crowd – then forgotten what it was. I waited for him to be removed or just wander off again but he stayed there, perched on a stool at the side of the stage, occasionally wandering over to the mic between numbers and burbling a bit about something or other. That's when I decided he must be something to do with the band – one of their mates that they felt sorry for or something.

It wasn't until I realised he was actually trying to introduce the songs that it dawned on me he was some sort of announcer, though he certainly didn't look like any telly announcer I had ever seen. Long, lank hair, scruffy-looking half-beard, just kind of standing there looking awkward in his round-collared denim shirt and split-coloured, flared loon pants. Then when he did manage to squeeze out a few coherent words about one of the songs, the band would laugh and proceed to play a different one, the whole thing gradually descending into a sort of non-presentational chaos.

Throughout it all, Peel looked on calmly, perfectly accepting of the apparent absurdity of the situation, obviously not that bothered about whether the folks at home were getting it or not. I remember not really knowing what to think. I didn't yet know his name or face well enough to recognise him as the odd one out who had mimed the part of the mandolin player when Rod and the boys did 'Maggie May' on *Top of the Pops*. I still thought he'd just beamed in from outer space somewhere. Then my mum, also forced into watching and sitting on the settee next to me, tutted loudly, and that's when I knew for sure that I quite liked this funny-looking bloke – parental disapproval, I had long since learned, being a sure sign of something interesting going on. When he mentioned that the band would also be appearing on his Radio 1 show later that month, I made a mental note to look out for it.

It took me about three weeks to find his show on the radio. I had gathered that he was not one of the regular daytime goons on Radio 1, but I was not familiar with any of their evening programmes yet. Instead, I was a veteran of Radio Luxembourg's FAB 208 station, which had such a wobbly signal that the station would routinely weave in and out of human hearing, but it played a lot of records that Radio 1 didn't, including songs that had even been banned by the BBC. (The current *bête noire* in 1972 was the Wings single 'Hi, Hi, Hi'. I remember tuning into Luxembourg specifically to hear it after Radio 1 had banned it for its 'licentious lyrics'. Fantastic!) It wasn't until I started searching for the Peel programme that I realised there was a lot of good stuff on Radio 1 in the evenings. There was Alan Black and Annie Nightingale, who did a sort of review show, playing tracks from all the latest cool albums. I was puzzled to hear them describe the Faces as 'a great band that has never really captured their live sound on record'. I thought about it and decided, grudgingly, that they might have a point.

When I finally found the Peel show – which, I

discovered, was the last show Radio 1 would broadcast most weekdays before shutting down for the night (it would be another twenty years before Radio 1 became a twenty-four-hour station) – I was lying in bed pretending to be asleep but with the transistor radio nestling on the pillow by my ear. Unable to check the wavelength in the dark, I thought I had accidentally tuned into some foreign station playing jazz or something. I was just about to carry on turning the dial when I heard his voice. 'Matching Mole,' he said. 'But then you probably knew that ...'

Right. I carried on listening but, unlike at least some of the stuff on Bob Harris and Annie Nightingale, I didn't recognise a single thing he played. I wondered where all this music I knew nothing about had come from, and what it all meant. I didn't even really like a lot of it, I just kept listening all the same, curious as to what bizarre thing he might play next. Then suddenly he played the sublime 'Mandolin Wind' from Rod Stewart's solo album *Every Picture Tells a Story*. 'Possibly the finest song I think young Roderick has ever written,' I recall him sighing deeply at the end of it – an opinion I had already formed myself. That was the moment I became hooked. Despite appearances, this Peel bloke seemed to know what he was talking about.

The next night I lay in bed with the radio pressed to my ear again. I waited for him to play another Rod Stewart or Faces track but he never did. Instead he played a session from a new group called Roxy Music. I had never taken drugs – didn't even know what drugs looked like or what shops you bought them from – but this, to me, definitely sounded like music made by people who took drugs. It was long, way out and hard to follow, but it drew me in like a science-fiction novel that I couldn't put down. I saved up two weeks' worth of paper-round money – £2.50 – in order to buy their first album, the one with the white cover with the sultry space-vixen on it.

And so it began ... Or rather, that's how it began for me, this special relationship I would develop in my mind with John Peel. I was hardly the first. Though I didn't know it yet, by then Peel had already influenced at least two generations of music fans and helped kick-start the careers of some of the biggest and best rock artists of the age, from Hendrix to Bowie and all points in between. And, of course, I would hardly be the last. Indeed, ask any former listeners under the age of thirty-five what the Peel show meant to them and they will point to him as the man who brought the world such names as Joy Division, the Smiths, and the Fall. While in more recent times, with many of his listeners now young enough to be his grandchildren – right to the end the Peel show attracted the highest percentage of listeners under the age of sixteen of any show on Radio 1 – he would no doubt be best known as the fatherly-type dude who gave us the Strokes and the White Stripes.

Whatever the entry point into the Peel musical story, however, the result has nearly always been the same: a vague feeling of repellence at first, perhaps, tinged with a slightly morbid curiosity, followed soon after, if you dared to persist, by the warm inner glow of understanding, and then, if you hung around too long, sudden and complete addiction. It was something you could shake off temporarily, perhaps, but never quite leave behind. Over the last ten years of his life, it was discovered, in fact, that a high percentage of regular listeners to his Radio 1 show were people who had first listened to it as teenagers or students, and were now coming back to it again in later life.

I am the living proof of this. A middle-aged father whose daughters now tell me what to play in the car, when I was driving alone at night, I would sometimes still find Peel on the radio and turn the volume up as far as it would go without distorting – not always easy to judge on a Peel show. Trundling through the countryside on my way home from London, scaring the wildlife for miles around as the monstrous sound of the Fall doing their thousandth session came blaring out of the carelessly opened windows, it was always fantastically comforting to know that old Peely was still out there doing it, come shit or shine. The rest of us might have had to grow up and get used to knowing far more about Britney Spears or *EastEnders* (thanks, kids) than we could ever want to, but not, thank God, John Peel. It had long since ceased being important whether I liked every record he played; I just adored the fact that he was still playing them. Often, I still wondered vaguely as I tried tuning in while driving in the dark whether I hadn't accidentally alighted on some distant signal broadcasting from an ancient Buddhist retreat in the Himalayas. But by now I would have been disappointed not to have thought that from time to time. It was, after all, one of the things his show did best: surprise you, make you think.

I had remained an avid listener long after I no longer needed to hide under the bedclothes to be one. I grew up, left school and paid close attention as his show suddenly changed, in the summer of 1976, into something else again, something new. Peel was suddenly sounding excited again and the reason was a wave of new British bands then starting to emerge under the banner of something called punk rock. It didn't matter whether you liked it or not, soon almost everybody and everything seemed to be infected by it. As a result, I bought my first pair of straight-legged jeans that year, then dyed my hair black and had it cut into a spiky approximation of Johnny Rotten's hairstyle. I can't thank – or blame – Peel for that. But it was John's fault that I also bought Patti Smith's *Horses* album that year, followed by the first Ramones album, then later the first Damned, Clash, Jam and Pistols singles, and, most marvellous of all, or so it seemed to me back then, the first Television album, *Marquee Moon*.

Mark P of Peel show regulars Alternative TV, who I later worked with in the late seventies at his independent label, Step Forward Records, had famously shown the three basic guitar chords – E, A, D – in the original punk fanzine he started in '76, *Sniffin' Glue*, adding the caption: 'Now go and form a band!' Now it seemed as though the youth of the entire country had taken his advice to heart and formed a band. I was never in a band but I was still intoxicated by the DIY ethos of punk and when the weekly music paper *Sounds* ran an ad looking for new writers – adding the magic words: 'no experience necessary' – I took it as a sign and immediately applied.

I didn't get the job but they did invite me to try my hand at reviewing some live shows for them on a freelance basis. I thought of Bowie at the Empire Pool, Wembley, where I had seen him on the 'Station To Station' tour the year before, I remembered all the tickets for Clash and Sex Pistols shows I'd never been able to get, and immediately said yes. For my first review, they sent me to a pub called the Red Cow in Hammersmith, then one of the most seedy and decrepit parts of west London, to watch a group I had never heard of called the Lurkers. Disenchanted and fearing the worst, I was surprised by how taken I was with the whole thing, the band sounding not unlike a more junior, more English version of the Ramones.

When the review ran in *Sounds*, in October 1977, I still knew nothing about the group, but when I saw the review in the paper, all set out in neat typescript with a picture and headline, it looked as if I was some sort of expert. It was thrilling – and rather odd. But not as odd as actually receiving a cheque in the post a few weeks later. I had been paid £12. For writing a review. Published in *Sounds*. Standing there with that cheque in my hand, staring at it, I could not imagine how anything could possibly get better than this.

Then a few nights later something happened that made all the excitement of suddenly being a 'published writer' momentarily evaporate. I was listening to Peel in my bedroom as usual when I suddenly heard it. At first I wasn't sure but then he said it again – my name! He was talking about the Lurkers, and the gist of it, as far as I could make out in my hysteria over hearing my name on the radio, was that until he read my recent review he had believed he was the only person in the music biz who liked the Lurkers. He then played a Lurkers track. God knows what it was called but right then it sounded like the greatest two minutes of my life. John Peel had mentioned me on his show! Now I could die happy. Well, almost. The trouble was, nobody else I knew had heard it, so rather than being able to bask in the expected glory, I found myself looked on with suspicion if not complete contempt by doubting friends. As one kindly Sid Vicious clone I used to know put it: '*Your* name? On *Peel*? Bollocks!'

After a while, devoid of positive reinforcement, I even began doubting myself. Had I really heard *my* name on the John Peel show? Bollocks ... I never mentioned it again, and only do so now to illustrate how much such a meagre morsel meant to a teenager still trying to find his way in the world, looking to make some sort of mark, however small and insignificant to others – and to imagine then what it must have felt like to actually be in a band that had a record or – holiest of grails – a session played on his show. Could there be a bigger accolade?

The only person who ever remembered my instantly forgettable little name-check was John himself. I first glimpsed him in the *Sounds* office one day in the summer of 1978. He was delivering his weekly column at the same time as I happened to be dropping off my latest 250-word masterpiece. He had just returned from the pub with the editor, Alan Lewis, and seemed suitably good-humoured, so I decided on the spur of the moment to risk a small intrusion. As he waved goodbye to Alan and made his way to the lift in the corridor, I followed him. I stood next to him while he waited for the lift to arrive and saw him glance at me quizzically out of the corner of his eye.

'Mr Peel,' I said.

'John,' he said.

'John ...'

'Yes?'

The lift doors opened and he stepped inside. I stayed where I was. He looked at me expectantly. It was now or never.

'John Peel!' I blurted.

'Yes,' he said, beginning to show faint signs of alarm.

'Mick Wall,' I said, holding out my hand.

'Ah, yes,' he said, shaking it warmly. 'The Lurkers fan, unless I'm very much mistaken ...'

I winced. The lift doors began to close as I stood there nodding like a fool. Like a Lurkers fan, in fact – which is how, as the years slid by and I was fortunate enough to run into him again occasionally, I became known to him whenever we met.

Appearing as a guest on the Andy Kershaw show some ten years later, for example, I bumped into John in the corridor at Radio 1 one afternoon as we were both making our way towards the drinks machine. I said hello and the first thing he said was: 'Whatever happened to the Lurkers then?' I shrugged and shook my head. 'Never mind,' he said consolingly. I tried to get myself a large white coffee with sugar but I couldn't get that right, either. 'Here,' said John, taking my Styrofoam cup, 'allow me ...' The coffee came and it tasted good, as brought to me by John Peel. At the end of the day, I thought, how many Lurkers fans can say that?

The last time I ever saw John in the flesh was backstage at the Glastonbury Festival a few years ago. I was on my way out of the 'New Tent', overloaded by angst-ridden caterwauling and tragically detuned, disproportionately loud guitars. John was on his way in, eager-eyed and mental antennae twitching. It was raining (of course) and he was wearing the usual anorak and wellies.

'What's going on in there?' he asked.

'Oh God,' I sighed, 'I don't know ... something noisy.'

'Sounds promising,' he said.

I watched him stroll off into the tent, the crowd visibly parting for him as he took up a position about halfway down to one side, his head wagging gently as the band attempted spontaneous combustion on the stage. 'Jesus,' I thought, 'how does he do it?' Then I went off to look for all the other music-weary travellers in the backstage bar.

Listening figures have declined for Radio 1 over recent years, as with every other form of 'traditional' media in the new multi-channel, digitised age. The advent of commercial radio, MTV, the internet and mobile phones that speak your weight has steadily eaten into the heart of Radio 1's daytime listenership. Record sales are dramatically down too, we are told, and of course no one watches *Top of the Pops* any more, let alone tapes it.

But one thing had always remained unchanged about British broadcasting – or at least it had, until 25 October 2004, the real day the music died – and that was the John Peel show. His listening figures rarely changed. If anything, in recent years they had begun to go up again. However high-tech your laptop, however media-savvy your set-up, however many zillions of downloads, MP3s, old-fashioned bootlegs and rare collected box-set editions you possess, until now there still remained only one place on earth where you could hear what we can only call the Music of John Peel. Because that's what it was. The things he chose to play, the way he played them straight after things they apparently had no relationship to whatsoever – that was the Music of John Peel, and that's what we were all really listening to every time we were fortunate enough to catch one of his immaculately dishevelled shows. The sort of music, as Paul Hartnoll of Orbital later pointed out, 'you would sort of end up loving – by default, because he loved it so much.'

I also met Peel's redoubtable producer, John Walters, a couple of times in the 1980s. Unfortunately, the first time we met, in about 1981, at some club gig in London (the name of the band entirely escapes me), I was introduced to him by a well-meaning but clearly misguided friend as 'the best young writer on *Sounds*'.

'Harrumph,' he scowled, 'well, that's not saying much, is it?' Then he strode off, pint in hand, his good works to perform.

He was right, of course, but that didn't mean he had to be rude about it. I admit that for a while after that it was impossible to hear a Peel show without feeling somewhat let down. Years later, however, when we met again under more convivial circumstances, Walters would explain that he had had 'a particular bee in my bonnet at that time about *Sounds* because of the appalling way they had treated John'. Some months before, John had resigned from his column after the paper's then resident punk-priest, Dave McCullough, had begun making unwarranted comments about him in the paper.

I told him to forget about it. Sitting with him in a pub round the corner from the Radio 1 office at Egton House that he and Peel had shared for over fifteen years at that point, you could forgive him anything as he settled, over the inevitable pint, into telling me about his role not just as producer of the show but as the veritable keeper of the Peel flame; the *éminence grise* behind the success of the show who constantly watched the DJ's back.

'The thing the powers that be at the good old BBC don't realise,' I recall him saying, 'is that the Peel show is probably the best programme the station has ever had. They'd laugh at me if they heard me say that but you wait and see. To me, John is like the Van Gogh of broadcasting. I don't mean he's only got one ear, I mean people think he's only interested in the strange and the obscure. But years from now, after we're both dead and buried, you mark my words, they'll be saying John Peel was the greatest DJ who ever lived and why can't there be more like him now!'

I had no idea how prophetic Walters' words would be. Instead, when I stopped off at his office later that day and found him sitting there fiddling with his trumpet (he had begun his career as a trumpet player in the Alan Price Set and still kept it in the office), it was hard to imagine there would ever come a day when he and Peel would be 'dead and buried'.

Well, that day has finally come. Walters died in July 2001 and John, of course, passed away after a heart attack while on holiday in Peru with his wife, Sheila, in October 2004.

Like one of his much-cherished red wines, John matured nicely with age. When he held his first grandchild, Archie, for the first time: 'The tears rolled down my face apparently from nowhere.' And where once he had auctioned his kidney stone for charity just minutes after painfully passing it while DJ-ing at a student party; just before he died he filmed a TV ad for the National Blood Service's latest campaign to help attract donors, a subject close to his heart since, as he says in the ad, 'Without this woman, my wife Sheila would have died after giving birth to our son.'

Of course, mentioning his family on air became another hallmark of all his shows on Radio 1, and again later, in the late nineties, when he began presenting his award-winning *Home Truths* programme on Radio 4. On air, particularly on *Home Truths*, he would let us into his private world, one of teenage children who littered their untidy bedrooms with pizza boxes and Game Boys, and a wife who he was devoted to, fondly addressed as the Pig, and celebrated her 'wrapping her body around mine even on the warmest nights.' (He even wore a large silver ring with a pig on it on his wedding finger as a sign of his 'big love'.) Nevertheless, their problems and endearments were the same as everybody else's. As the kids were growing up, he once recalled that 'when the two older ones [William and Alexandra] were seven and eight they banged on my door and said, "Dad, could you turn the records down?" I thought, this isn't the way it's supposed to be...' He said he never knew if they ever really listened to his programmes. 'It would be nice to think they did occasionally, though.' Apart from the opening lyric to 'Teenage Kicks', there was one epitaph he had recently admitted he would actually prefer: 'Quite a good dad'.

But if Peel's commitment to music remained singular – a former member of the Eddie Grundy fan club and lifelong fan of *The Archers* (even appearing in one episode, as himself) strolling round the family farmhouse in Suffolk in an Extreme Noise Terror T-shirt and what looked like his grandmother's cardigan – over the last six years of his life, his work on *Home Truths* introduced him to a whole new set of listeners, a great many of whom had never heard his Radio 1 show and had no previous connection with him. No matter, they soon came to love and look forward each week to his warm, amazingly perceptive, often funny, mostly melancholy stories about 'ordinary people that have led extraordinary lives, for one reason or another.'

John Peel was also the living proof of the difference between the BBC and its commercial rivals. His was a genuinely public-service programme. As a result, in over thirty-seven years at the BBC he was never once approached to work for a rival commercial station. 'I used to get this loyalty payment from the BBC,' he recalled. 'But then I think it dawned on them that no one else was trying to seduce me.'

Certainly the programmes he made for both Radio 1 and Radio 4 adhered to what might be termed Reithian principles: often giving you what was good for you rather than what you actually craved. Plus, no commercial station would have taken the chance of alienating its advertisers by having someone who pointedly refused to consult the Top Thirty when choosing the music for his shows. John's belief in public-service broadcasting was also clearly evident from his long-standing commitment to the BBC's World Service, for whom he presented a weekly music programme for more than twenty years.

He also wrote well – contributing articles over the years to countless newspapers and magazines around the world. His witty, often surreal weekly column in the seventies for *Sounds* is still fondly recalled by those of us who read it. Later pieces for the *Observer* showed just how erudite and perceptive he was. While, most brilliantly, in recent years, his regular weekly column in the *Radio Times* focused more on the quirks of family life.

Nevertheless, right to the end of his life, Peel was reluctant to relinquish his outpost at the cutting edge of popular taste, featuring 'anything and everything – as long as it's good'. A simple yet hard-to-define motto. For Peel, 'good' could be, as he said, almost anything. Of the twenty-two eager young disc jockeys who the BBC hired as the first generation of presenters on Radio 1 in 1967, the one for whom no sane person would have predicted a lasting career with the corporation was the nonconformist Peel. Yet while all the others either fell by the wayside or became bloated figures of ridicule to a young audience, it was the wilfully idiosyncratic Peel who would go on to become an institution within the corporation and, in time, the nation as a whole.

And yet he never played on that reputation. Unlike other Radio 1 DJs, he wasn't interested in a career on

TV presenting game shows. After his falling-out with Marc Bolan in the seventies, he never even really spent much time with the artists he devoted so many years of his shows to. As John once told Paul Morley, 'I think knowing amazingly few people in bands helps me keep my perspective. But when I get to see the Undertones, all reason deserts me.' And, of course, he kicked open the door at Radio 1 for people like Steve Lamacq, Jo Whiley, Mark Radcliffe, Mark Lamarr and, most particularly, the 'sorcerer's apprentice' Andy Kershaw – proving time after time to successive generations of BBC programmers that an audience existed for music that was not always a chart fixture.

Subtly influencing the rise of almost every style of popular music that has emerged over the past four decades, he disliked discussing all the bands he had discovered or given their first national radio play to. He didn't see it, he said, as 'notches on my bedpost'. He had 'just been doing my job'. Artists like Captain Beefheart, David Bowie, the Smiths, New Order, Pulp and the White Stripes had 'discovered themselves,' he said. John had done no more than merely shine a torchlight on them. And he was always careful to give a mention of whatever tiny label the record he had just played had been released on. 'Glasgow's finest, I'm told,' he would comment, dryly.

His almost supernatural modesty, his hard-fought 'ordinariness' – the wry, laconic delivery, the soft but unflinching Liverpudlian burr – were a huge part of his appeal. Paunchy and balding even in the mid-seventies, he would grow into a badly dressed middle age the envy of spivved-up punk tykes half his age. 'You'll have to believe me when I say I don't work at my appearance,' he said.

'I hate it,' he said, 'when they say I'm a national institution because, to me, they're things covered in ivy.' But that's what John Peel had become long before he was suddenly snatched from us. Until then, I had just assumed he would always be there. He was the fourth emergency service – the one fixed point on the dial in a world otherwise gone utterly mad. What other DJ could lay claim to having been the first to play Leonard Cohen in the 1960s – and the White Stripes in the twenty-first century? One story has him listening attentively to the BBC TV test tone, a steady pulse of electronic buzzing, and commenting ruefully, 'That sounds like something I might play on my show.'

Famously, of course, his favourite record of all time was 'Teenage Kicks' by the Undertones, who were signed by Sire Records pretty much straight after Peel played their home-produced EP for the first time on his show – twice! His enthusiasm was returned by the Undertones. As singer Feargal Sharkey says: 'I owe my life to John Peel.'

Gillian Reynolds wrote in the *Telegraph*: 'Honesty, integrity, a kind heart, perfect manners and a gently questing intelligence were qualities that would have given John Peel a place of his own in any profession. In the music business, where fashions change faster than the weather, they were quite extraordinary.'

Peel always regretted that he was unable to sing himself. As he once said, 'Making a noise like a dolphin is a very poor substitute.' But he made up for it by somehow managing to appear both enduringly adolescent and old before his time. Relentlessly professional, yet clearly not on the payroll of any record company, his recommendations carried real weight. Time and again, music that seemed marginal when Peel first enthused about it came to be accepted as being at the heart of the history of pop.

Ultimately, John Peel proved that it wasn't only teenagers who resented being told what to do, who knew how to rebel. As he once wryly acknowledged: 'My knowledge is overrated. I've never had a great memory and I'm shit on LP titles.'

As BBC director of radio and music Jenny Abramsky said the day his death was announced: 'John Peel was a unique broadcaster whose influence on Radio 1 could be felt from its very first days. He nurtured musicians and listeners alike, introducing them to new sounds. His open-minded approach to music was mirrored by his equally generous approach to his audience when he [also] went to Radio 4 to present *Home Truths*. He had a remarkable rapport with all his listeners. Everyone at BBC Radio is devastated by the news. John is simply irreplaceable. Our hearts go out to Sheila and his children.'

This, then, is my affectionate portrait and appreciation of the life and times of the most highly regarded, influential music presenter in the history of British radio – John Peel, OBE. A close personal friend to millions, who will be greatly missed by us all ...

Mick Wall
Oxfordshire, November, 2004

CHAPTER ONE

From Woodlands to
The Perfumed Garden

Unexpectedly, for a man whose professional reputation was built on his no-nonsense, anti-showbiz approach, John Peel was not John's real name but an on-air nom de plume. Nor did he later change it by deed poll, as has sometimes been suggested in the past. He was, in fact, born John Robert Parker Ravenscroft in Heswall, near Liverpool, on 30 August 1939. He was brought up on the Wirral – the son of Robert Bob Ravenscroft, stern, upper-middle-class scion of the family cotton business.

John later complained that his childhood had been blighted by distant parents who used their wealth to build a wall between him and his two younger brothers, Alan and Frank. His father had spent the duration of the Second World War stationed in North Africa as an officer in the army. As a result, John was six years old before he was introduced to his father in person. Until then a solitary and wistful child, it had come as a huge shock to have this larger-than-life, authoritarian figure suddenly running the household. They rarely saw eye to eye on anything – least of all John's interest in music, which his father deplored and ridiculed – and the uncomfortable relationship they endured was to leave its mark on him. It was, John ventured later in life, perhaps one of the reasons why he had tried so hard to be a fair and non-judgemental father to his own children.

His mother, meanwhile, offered even less emotional support. She was the product of a well-to-do family from Preston, and John would later characterise her as a regular 'tippler' who remained as distant a figure to him and his brothers as their father. Lost for much of the time in an alcoholic fug, 'she didn't seem to know what we were for,' he later observed. He had the impression that his mother had been 'frightened of me from the moment I was born.' Instead, he was brought up almost entirely by a live-in nanny, and when as a young boy he rode his beloved tricycle through a greenhouse window, it did not even occur to either the stuff-and-nonsense nanny or his inebriated mother to bother to apply anaesthetic while his wounds were being hastily stitched up.

It was an eccentric, 'animals first, children second' environment typical of the gentrified classes of the time. Years later, John would make up all sorts of stories about his 'weird and wonderful' family, some true, some possibly less so. He once told his Radio 1 producer and close friend, John Walters, that his grandfather used to receive champagne free on the National Health. Always one to pick holes in everything, Walters replied that he could scarcely believe him and that Peel must have been having his leg pulled by his grandfather when he told him that one. A few days later, however, Peel returned to the subject. 'Oh, I asked my mum,' he told Walters, 'and I muddled it up. It wasn't champagne. It was morphine.'

Despite the warm Liverpudlian burr he allowed to inflect his vowels as a broadcaster, as he once confessed, John was 'not a proper Scouser at all.' He had actually grown up on the opposite side of the River Mersey, in Heswall, where all the wealthy Liverpool folk retreated at night, and as a child he spoke with an impeccably cut-glass accent in keeping with his upper-crust Cheshire upbringing.

John's father's office was in Liverpool and his mother would do most of the family shopping there, too. He would accompany her regularly on these trips, not because he enjoyed shopping with his mother but because of the opportunity it afforded him to experience what he saw then as the Big City, crossing on the same creaking old ferry that Gerry & the Pacemakers would later make famous in song.

John was eight when he first fell in love with football, with the reconvening of the English professional leagues after the war. Liverpool, famously, were always his team. He dreamed of playing for them long before he ever dreamed of anything else, and was still dreaming, he once said, 'long past the point of feasibility.'

By then he was a boarder at Woodlands prep school in Deganwy, north Wales, where his father had sent him when he was just seven. 'At the school I went to I was the only Liverpool supporter and I think everyone else, except for one boy who didn't like football, supported Manchester United,' was his chief recollection from those days.

At fourteen, he was sent to board at Shrewsbury, one of the most highly regarded (and expensive) public schools in England, where he arrived a couple of years after fellow 'Old Salopians', as former pupils are called, such as Willie Rushton, Richard Ingrams and Paul Foot, later founders of the satirical magazine *Private Eye*, and not long before future *Monty Python* star Michael Palin.

Being sent to Shrewsbury was by then almost a family tradition. John's father and both grandfathers had also previously been pupils there. John, however, hated the place from the moment he arrived. Still the same shy, lonely boy, he now began to show a streak of budding adolescent obstinacy, if not downright nonconformity. It was an attitude guaranteed to bring him the wrong kind of attention and he paid for his 'irregularity' in regular thrashings from both prefects and masters. The school authorities, he once recalled with dismay, 'practically had to wake [me] up during the night in order to administer the required number of sound beatings.' He said he estimated the flagellation rate in his first term alone at approximately 'once every three days,' with at least thirty floggings just for forgetfulness.

He added, tongue in cheek, that when he was thirteen he was 'rather lovely' to look at and 'much sought after by older boys who, if they developed an appetite for you, could have you beaten on a number of pretexts.' Several of these older boys, he suggested mischievously, went on to enjoy considerable success and even eminence in the business world. 'I'm sometimes tempted to turn up with a little rouge on my cheeks and say "I'm ready for you now, my angel" to some ageing captain of industry,' he remarked only half-jokingly.

On a more serious level, John later claimed that the only reason he was able to survive the ordeal of life at Shrewsbury was because of his discovery, as a teenager, of first Elvis Presley and then, just two weeks later, Little Richard. 'I stared open-mouthed,' he remembered. 'I had never heard anything so raw, so elemental.' After which, 'my whole life changed, it really did. I don't think I was ever quite the same person again. Everything changed when I first heard Elvis. Where there had been nothing there was suddenly something.'

In time, his enthusiasm for music would surpass even his passion for Liverpool FC, but his interest hadn't really been sparked until then. The first concert he had ever been taken to as a child was a performance in Liverpool by the Obernkirchen Children's Choir, the highlight of which had been their enthused chanting of 'Val-da-ree, val-da-rah', he remembered.

Now, at Shrewsbury, he acquired his first wireless, on which he would listen avidly every night to more glamorous, distant radio programmes than the staid BBC had to offer, which in the 1950s consisted mainly of programmes like *Housewives' Choice* – housewives still then considered a separate breed to the rest of society. On TV, new pop and rock shows like *Oh Boy!* were soon to have their own impact but television was still something frowned on by the housemasters at Shrewsbury and John wouldn't get to see much television until he went to live in America a couple of years later.

He was particularly fond of the American Forces Network in Europe, then broadcasting out of Stuttgart, and the early Radio Luxembourg broadcasts – utterly raucous by BBC standards, more thrillingly American in tone, and where the signal was always 'satisfyingly feeble', giving one the feeling of belonging to a strange but select club. Just like the many millions of young school-age listeners who would first come across his own nightly shows on Radio 1 while huddled in the dark under the bedclothes, the transistor pressed to their ears, John used to listen to the radio while lying in bed at night, trying to ignore his oppressive dormitory surroundings, the radio taking him to exotic, faraway places unobtainable in any other way to a teenage boy still waiting to get his kicks.

He began spending most of his allowance on records. 'I had started listening a bit to Radio Luxembourg, then I heard Elvis Presley doing "Heartbreak Hotel" on Two-Way Family Favourites [on the BBC].' It was, he said, 'quite literally transcendental.' The kind of magical moment 'my children will never experience'. When he then heard Little Richard, it was 'like Saul on the road to Damascus. Literally, nothing was ever the same in my life again.'

Apart from Elvis, Little Richard, Gene Vincent and the rest of the original generation of American rockers, John also loved British skiffle star Lonnie Donegan, whose mid-fifties hit 'Rock Island Line' he later compared favourably with anything by Elvis of the same period. John would have the pleasure of meeting Lonnie many years later, at the Holiday Inn in Nottingham, three days before he died. John later wrote of him in the *Guardian*: 'Lonnie Donegan – the man whose first hit crucially predated Elvis's first hit by four months; the man whose work so irritated my father that he attempted, in turn, to irritate me by always referring to him as "Lolly Dolligan"; the man who, for me, pressed the start button on a life of at times irrational pleasure in popular music.'

He was fifteen when he first began to fantasise about

what fun it would be to be the one actually spinning the records on his beloved radio. 'I had records [but] no one to play them to, I thought playing them on the radio would be wonderful. And of course, it is.'

He still believed that the DJs played only the records they personally wanted to hear, 'and I thought that there was a job that I wanted to do. But there didn't seem to be much possibility of me doing it at the time. My father told me that I couldn't get a job on the BBC unless I was Catholic or homosexual or both. He had a rather distorted view of life, I think. Nice chap but funny views.' Undeterred, John had actually written to Pete Murray, asking how to become a DJ. 'But he didn't answer.' (When they later came to work together on the fledgling Radio 1, Peel reminded Murray of the letter but the smooth-talking BBC veteran claimed never to have received it. Interestingly, however, speaking on Radio 2 a couple of weeks after John's death, Murray said he now remembered the letter and actually replied with advice. 'John was frightfully posh, you know,' he said, 'spoke like that. He wrote to me when he was at Shrewsbury ... There were no local BBC stations in those days so I recommended he work for hospital radio. Learn your trade, I said.')

While John's enthusiasm for both football and music would continue to grow with the years, his academic studies left a lot to be desired, he confessed. Memories of trying to get his dreamy thoughts focused on trigonometry – a pet hate at school – were still likely to induce headaches. 'It just wouldn't penetrate at all,' he said. 'They'd tell me I was going to need this later in life, and I used to say: "I can assure you I will never do anything that requires trigonometry."'

Eventually failing more exams than he passed, sixteen-year-old John Ravenscroft emerged from Shrewsbury with just four O levels, and even then one of them was 'disputed' – his Divinity exam, which for some reason he was granted even though he only got eleven per cent after writing the answers 'in the style of Damon Runyon'. He claimed he discovered this anomaly many years later when his mother had given him all his old end-of-school reports just before she died. He did, however, make sure he left Shrewsbury having obtained his house football colours.

His housemaster at Shrewsbury, R.H.J. Brooke, whom John later described as 'extraordinarily eccentric' but 'amazingly perceptive', wrote prophetically on his final school report: 'Perhaps it's possible that John can form some kind of nightmarish career out of his enthusiasm for unlistenable records and his delight in writing long and facetious essays.'

John's father had other ideas, however, and planned for his eldest son – and heir – to follow him into the family business once he'd returned to Heswall. Concerned, though, by his son's puzzling lack of enthusiasm for this idea, as John later recalled, his father instead 'shrewdly got me a job working for one of his competitors' at a cotton mill in Rochdale owned by a family friend. By now, however, John's parents had separated – his mother moving to a luxury apartment in London – and he was glad to get out of the house now solely occupied by his father. Despite never having been close to his parents, John confided to friends in later life that coming home from school to find his mother gone was a devastating blow that he would struggle to come to terms with for many years.

Life outside work was a drudge, too. Musically, there was little of note happening in the mid-1950s, at least not in Liverpool, and certainly not in Rochdale and its grim environs. London was still the only place in the country where the big American stars of radio ever performed in Britain, and even then only in small, war-rationed doses. Post-austerity, pre-rock'n'roll, the biggest stars the Liverpool Empire saw were anodyne mums-and-dads singers like Johnnie Ray and Frankie Laine, saccharine American pop stars who lots of girls appeared to like but who held little or no appeal for the increasingly restless young Ravenscroft.

With only a large, empty house inhabited by an increasingly disapproving father to go home to at night, John began helping out as a part-time volunteer at a working-class boys' club in a run-down district of Liverpool – largely because, he later claimed ruefully, it had two indoor football pitches. His father was predictably 'mystified' if not downright appalled at this latest turn of events, finding his eldest son mixing with hoi polloi. Disgusted by what he perceived as John's shocking lack of ambition, he took to introducing him to visitors as 'the idiot of the family'. When John simply ignored him and continued his activities at the club, his father went so far as to warn him that he was concerned his son was developing an 'unhealthy interest' in young boys.

'They took the mickey out of my accent but they were really kind to me,' Peel later recalled of his time at the boys' club. 'Coming from a family where it was considered the worst possible taste to show any affection for your wife or your children, I liked it. And I liked the football.'

John's father did manage to instil in him one mutual interest, though: the automobile. His father owned a fleet of 'rather exotic cars', including, at various junctures, a Citroën Traction Avant, a Minerva, and a rare Morgan three-wheeler. Two of three Talbot 105s that had been specially built for a race at Brooklands were also once owned by his father. John also had a couple of aunts on his father's side who collected vintage cars. As a result, he recalled being taken as a child for a drive through the countryside in a Bugatti that had once belonged to Sir Malcolm Campbell, the fabled British racing driver who held the world land and water speed records in the 1920s and 1930s, and later became the first man to drive a car at over 300 mph. Campbell had won the 1927 and 1928 Grand Prix de Boulogne driving a Bugatti T39A, and was exactly the sort of glamorous, gung-ho character the teenage Ravenscroft very much approved of. Like Elvis on four wheels. As a result, despite his genuinely humble demeanour in later life, John's guiltily concealed passion for smart, expensive cars would stay with him for ever, though it would be some time before he would be able to afford one to match any of his father's.

In 1957, at the age of eighteen, John received his official call-up papers and left the family home again – not for the plush surrounds of a public school this time, however, but for the wooden-bunk, spit-and-make-do of the Royal Artillery regiment boot camp. As part of the National Service that was still the lot of all able-bodied young men back then, John spent from 1957 to 1959 in the Royal Artillery – as a B2 Radar operator – as well as playing goalkeeper for the regimental hockey team. In keeping with the almost creakingly modest figure he would cut after he became famous, the young gunner was inordinately proud – almost perversely so, thought some of his superiors – to be the only public schoolboy in the history of his regiment not to be appointed an officer.

It was also during his time in the army that John first began to consciously lose his posh Cheshire accent. In common with his wilfully underachieving performance at school, there was a streak of obstinacy, of passive-aggressive rebellion, in the pleasure he took at not ascending the red-carpeted ladder being offered him. As John would later recall, with great amusement and pride, his CO wrote on his final report: 'At no time has he shown any sign of adapting to the military way of life.' 'I took it as a compliment,' he deadpanned.

Just like Elvis, when John got out of the army in 1959 he found the world much changed. But where Elvis would never again scale the heights he had reached with his music before his strength-sapping stint in the US army, John was about to enter one of the most eventful periods of his life. By then, even Liverpool was undergoing the first stirrings of a dramatic new cultural shift that would literally change everything for John, and everybody else, as the foggy fifties became the swinging sixties.

Rock'n'roll had well and truly arrived and with it for the first time the concept of the 'teenager'. Now the old Empire was suddenly jumpin' to a whole new kind of kick and John would later recall seeing acts there for the first time like Clyde McPhatter, Duane Eddy, Eddie Cochran and, best of all, his beloved, leather-clad Gene Vincent. Vincent's career in America had peaked with million-selling hits like 'Be-Bop-A-Lula' and 'Lotta Lovin'', and was now on the wane. In entertainment-starved Britain, however, he was, briefly, the biggest live draw in the country. Seeing him play at the Empire had 'a very considerable effect on my life,' John said. 'I thought he was just astonishing.'

In terms of home-grown artists, however, there appeared to be few if any of comparable quality. 'You might get Joe Brown coming up now and then, but that was about it.' He was not aware that just a few miles up the road there was a group of young musicians who were about to change all that, then operating fitfully under the name the Silver Beatles.

In 1960, however, his life would be turned upside down again when his father, who had recently remarried and now wanted the house to himself and his new young bride, decided John would be better off trying his luck in the New World – Dallas, Texas, to be precise, where he was sent to 'learn the business' at a cotton company owned by yet another associate of his father. He stuck it out for a few months, struggling to become a computer programmer, then quit and for the next two years worked at a crop insurance company, before finally 'catching the wave', as he once put it, and throwing it all in to pursue a more haphazard but promisingly adventure-filled career as a disc jockey, as hip young American radio announcers now liked to be known.

Used to living away from home, John had quickly adjusted to his new life in America, a place he had always regarded with 'frank wonder' as the birthplace of Elvis and rock'n'roll. He even began to enjoy himself. Free at last from the stifling constraints of his gloomy home, John, now in his early twenties, came out of his shell for the first time and even started cracking jokes. He always had a wry take on everything, and seemed quite fearless for such a young man so far from home.

He bought his first American car – a 1958 Chevrolet Biscayne, which he later traded in for a 1961 model. He managed to drive that 'from Friendly Chevy in Dallas straight into the side of a truck.' When he wasn't wreaking havoc on the roads, he later recalled pleasant 'love romps on the edge of an orange grove' with a sweet-natured Texan belle named Manda. He also smoked grass for the first time, which some friends had brought back from a trip to Mexico. For a while, he was a regular visitor to a strip joint, where he was particularly taken by the nightly performances of a girl who went under the name of Chris Colt, the Girl with the 45s.

John was at work one afternoon in 1963 when news broke of the assassination of President John F. Kennedy. His office was just a few blocks away from the street with the soon-to-be-famous book repository opposite the now even more famous grassy knoll, so John decided to go down and take a look for himself, arriving within an hour of the shooting. But with police and besuited FBI men directing bystanders away from the scene, at first he couldn't get close enough to see anything of interest. He noticed, however, that police were letting reporters and photographers through the cordons and on the spur of the moment decided to present himself to the nearest policeman as a pressman from the *Liverpool Echo*, a very important newspaper in England. To his astonishment, this hastily contrived strategy, combined with his unmistakably 'foreign' accent, worked and even without credentials he was ushered straight through to the scene of the crime.

By then, however, there was little left to see, just the wide empty street as he'd seen it countless times before. The only thing that was different was the look on people's faces. After 'just standing around for a while taking it all in,' he returned to his office where he did actually try to phone in a report to the *Liverpool Echo*. He had assumed they would be ecstatic to have someone on the spot at such a history-making event. Instead, they barely ran a caption on the story. Even then, 'they wrote more about my dad than they did about me.'

Undeterred, John repeated his man-from-the-*Echo* stunt again that night, gaining entry to the press conference in the basement of the police headquarters in Dallas where the chief suspect, a handcuffed Lee Harvey Oswald, was paraded before reporters before being taken back to his cell and formally charged with the murder of the president.

When news was broadcast on TV the next day that Oswald had been shot and killed at a subsequent press conference by a shady character and self-appointed 'patriot' named Jack Ruby, 'I didn't know what to think,' said John. Describing it as 'only a brief brush with history,' he simply did not see it as a life-changing event in the way so many others plainly did.

And so things might have drifted along had fate not taken a hand. Objecting one afternoon to some woefully inaccurate piece of information about the Beatles given out on local radio station WRR, he actually phoned the station and had a conversation with the on-air DJ, Russ Knight, known to regular listeners as 'the Weird Beard'. Impressed as much by his English 'Beatles' accent as his 'expert' knowledge, Knight invited the young Englishman to come on his show more regularly to talk about the Beatles.

With Beatlemania then about to sweep the land, John was quick to realise that any vague approximation of a Liverpool accent would now accord the speaker a certain cachet with young American listeners. He discovered that the more he laid on the Scouse accent, the more often they asked him back onto the station, and throughout 1964 he became WRR's resident Beatles expert 'all the way from Liverpool, England!'

As he began to get comfortable in this new role, the bits John produced became wackier and the 'facts' he revealed increasingly unlikely – more than once he interviewed George Harrison, as played by himself. Almost overnight he began to be treated as a local celebrity, not least by the station's younger female listeners, the nasal pronunciation and short vowel sounds working as an unlikely aphrodisiac. He regaled friends back home with lascivious tales of his adventures. 'It was the glamour of the job,' he later admitted with a certain baffled glee. 'I was suddenly confronted by this succession of teenage girls who didn't want to know anything about me at all. All they wanted me to do was to abuse them, sexually, which of course I was only too happy to do.'

In retrospect, John would wave away his early success on US radio as 'pure luck', maintaining that anyone from England with a bit of ingenuity who found themselves in America at that time could have done the job just as well. 'They'd got this idea that if you lived in the UK there were probably only a couple of hundred people and they were all bound to know each other.' Meanwhile, he was gaining valuable experience of broadcasting on live radio. He was already developing his own laconic style, that prairie-dry sense of humour that would hold him in such good stead throughout his life and career.

His real break came when WRR decided to launch a late-night programme that soon became popular amongst Dallas teens called Kats' Karavan, an r&b show that featured mostly black music, even though the station's listenership was predominantly white. John was taken aback at how many of the kids out there appeared to love it, although, as he pointed out, 'if any of the musicians had turned up at their front door they would have called the police.'

John would regularly introduce the second hour of Kats' Karavan, chiefly because, he admitted, he had certain records the regular jocks at WRR didn't – specifically an LP by Lightnin' Hopkins, the famous Texas bluesman, which he had recorded for 77 Records, an obscure London-based label then operating out of Doug Dobell's shop on Charing Cross Road.

John's time in Dallas came to a suitably fly-by-night end after his love life became so entangled it actually began to endanger life and limb. He had recently been threatened with being run out of town at gunpoint by the father of a thirteen-year-old girl he had been caught with, though he insisted he thought she was older. Then, in 1965, obviously not yet of an age when learning from one's lessons is considered a priority, he took the astonishing step of marrying a fifteen-year-old girl named Shirley Anne Milburn. She was an orphan John had first got to know through her letters and calls to the station, but when he discovered that Shirley was about to be packed off to live hundreds of miles away with uncles she barely knew, he decided to intervene.

John always insisted that Shirley had sworn she was sixteen – as did the rest of her guardians and family – when he took pity and, as a way out of her predicament that met all the legal requirements, agreed to marry her.

John rarely spoke publicly of his marriage to Shirley. He did later claim, however, that neither of them ever saw the relationship as anything more than, quite literally, a marriage of convenience, going so far as to insist that they had never even consummated the union. It was, he tried his best to explain, more just a confused arrangement between two young and lonely people who didn't have anyone else to share their lives with at that point. John could relate to Shirley: in many ways, he felt like an orphan, too.

When he was offered the chance to present his own daily show – headhunted by the directors of KOMA in Oklahoma City, who fancied trying out some of that 'friend of the Beatles' stuff on their listeners, too – John jumped at it, packing his meagre belongings and several boxes of records into the battered Chevy and taking off the very next day. He had been in Dallas for four years.

When John left for Oklahoma, Shirley went with him – resulting in a potentially nasty run-in with the Dallas police who, unwilling at first to believe she was his wife, pointed out when they pulled him over for speeding that 'transporting a minor across state lines' was considered an even more serious offence in Texas. That was when John found out Shirley was still actually only fifteen, he said.

Possibly because they never defined the parameters of their feelings for each other, perhaps because there was such an age – and cultural – gap between them, the marriage, such as it was, was doomed to be an unstable and unhappy one. After John returned to London in the late sixties, he and Shirley lived in a flat in Fulham. But their falling-outs became infamous for their ferocity (Shirley would sometimes beat him up, he later claimed) and they had already lived apart for some time – John moving to a place of his own in Regent's Park – before they were finally divorced in 1973. Sad to relate, Shirley later served time in Holloway Prison for bank fraud. Not long after she was released, reportedly suffering from a severe bout of depression, Shirley committed suicide. It was one of the most fraught and painful episodes of Peel's life, and he referred to it in public not at all.

When John arrived at KOMA, the producers had the idea that he should drop the 's' from his name to make it easier for Americans to pronounce. So, typically unfazed, he began working as a full-time jock under the name 'John Ravencroft'. He stayed in Oklahoma for about eighteen months, finessing his style and his Beatles accent, then upped sticks again when he was invited to join the more glamorous KMEM radio in San Bernardino, southern California, where he would stay for another eighteen months. He began to earn good money and used some of it to buy himself a 1963 Chevy Impala. He'd only had it a few months, however, when he traded it in for the new 409 cubic-inch Super Sports model which had just come on the market. 'That was insanely powerful,' he recalled with no little relish. 'Most of them just blew up.'

John eventually lived in America for a total of seven years. Which meant, ironically, that he hadn't been around when the whole Merseybeat scene took off in Britain. Yet when he returned to London at the start of 1967, his long US sojourn had given him an aura of glamour. He had been the Englishman who had conquered American radio – an unheard-of achievement back then – and he had the rare record collection, the strange accent and the pretty seventeen-year-old Texan wife to prove it. Suddenly the shy retiring boy from Heswall had become positively exotic. More surprisingly, along with his new shoulder-length hairstyle and beard, it all rather suited him.

He also had a somewhat radical view of radio broadcasting – at least, by mid-sixties BBC standards. American radio may have been riddled with commercials, ID 'stings' and sponsor-plugs, but the actual chat was kept to the minimum and the records rattled out at an alarming speed. 'You were almost frightened to go to sleep in case you missed something,' John said. 'The stations were absolutely the centre of your life.'

Nevertheless, when he first returned to London he struggled, initially, to find work. America had hundreds of stations to pitch his wares to; Britain had only one: the BBC. Apart from the occasional, almost accidental infusion of some pop on programmes like good old *Two-Way Family Favourites*, and its embarrassingly popular younger Saturday-morning offshoot, *Children's Favourites*, BBC radio played hardly any modern music at all.

John's luck improved, however, when he met a businessman neighbour of his mother's who often placed advertising with Radio London, one of the new 'pirate' stations, so-called because they broadcast from ships anchored off the coast, just outside British territorial waters – a technicality that freed them of the needle-time restrictions that severely hampered the BBC's output. Pirates like Radio London and its only serious rival, Radio Caroline, were all the rage. He suggested John go and see Alan Keane, the programme controller at Radio London. John phoned Keane the next day and fixed an appointment to see him at the Radio London office. Once there, John explained that he'd been on the radio in California for three years and Keane 'just put me straight on the air without an audition or anything, for which I was extremely grateful.'

It was at Radio London – the 'Big L', as it became known to regular listeners – that John Ravenscroft became John Peel, from the old English folk song of the same name. It was a secretary at the station who suggested it, not for any cultural references, but simply because she thought it sounded snappier and more piratical than Ravenscroft. More important, from John's point of view, it was also classless. When he took the more proletarian-sounding 'Peel' as his name, John also symbolically discarded the last vestiges of his 'privileged' upbringing, allowing the Scouse to stay in his voice and, from this point on, distancing himself from any serious mention of his troubled early years.

Immediately slotted onto the daytime shift at Radio London, John also volunteered to do the midnight till two a.m. shift. It was to be a shrewd move. Correctly reasoning that few other people at the station would be listening at that time of night, John proceeded to tear up the playlist and started to spin some of the more interesting stuff he'd picked up on his travels in America by groups unknown to British ears, such as the Grateful Dead, Jefferson Airplane and Country Joe & the Fish.

Emboldened by the overjoyed response he started to get from listeners, John then took the unprecedented step of skipping all the ad breaks, weather reports and even the hourly news, so that he could play nothing but uninterrupted music. When Radio London producers found out what was going on they were furious. Then they took a look at the ratings and the music-press clippings and suddenly John was encouraged to develop the show.

Thus was born *The Perfumed Garden*, a suitably flower-powered name for a programme the likes of which had simply never been heard on British radio before. It was the first show on radio, pirate or otherwise, to showcase the new psychedelic sounds then emanating from the west coast of America, and a forerunner for every groundbreaking show he would later present for Radio 1. Mix-and-matching the fey, semi-mystical folk-rock musings of the Incredible String Band with the acid-laced, public school psychedelia of Syd Barrett's Pink Floyd, the proto-prog rock of the Third Ear Band and the 'pop' poetry of Adrian Mitchell, along with all sorts of musical 'happenings' live in the studio, including the first ever plays on British radio for both Captain Beefheart and Frank Zappa, by the summer of '67, John Peel and *The Perfumed Garden* would become as emblematic of the rapidly shifting times as anything released that summer by Hendrix, the Beatles or anyone else you'd dare to name.

British radio listeners had, quite literally, never heard anything like it. Segued by occasional stories from Peel himself apparently made up on the spot, and often as not about mice. Or men dressed as mice; or mice dressed as men. One was never quite sure. Certainly, the aptly named *Perfumed Garden* had more than a whiff of joss sticks about it. Showing the influence of his new best friend Marc Bolan, then singer- songwriter of whimsical folk rockers Tyrannosaurus Rex and another regular guest on the programme, on one early show John announced that 'the world is divided into two camps – Love and Hate, and Love will eventually win.'

He also began contributing articles to such infamous counterculture mags as *Gandalf's Garden* and the *International Times*, in one of which, typically, he earnestly advised readers to: 'Touch the bark of a thousand trees, shoeless ... then go to the children's playground in Kensington Gardens and stare at the elves on the trees there.' The sort of hydroponically charged space talk that would cause him a mixture of amusement and regret whenever reminded of it in later life. In another amusingly inappropriate column he would never have been able to get away with today, he described the sublime pleasures of squatting on Primrose Hill in the warm afternoon sunlight watching young schoolgirls glide by in their fetching summer uniforms.

But if Peel appeared as overcome by the conceits of the new post-acid age as any other idealistic young hippy, the most important factor behind his early success on the radio was that his style was immediately different to that of other presenters. He always made a point of playing the records from start to finish without talking all over them – exceedingly considerate for all those burgeoning home-tapers. When he spoke, it was as if he was speaking just to you – another unheard-of quality, most pirate DJs back then speaking as though to a crowd at a particularly noisy party. And to his growing band of regular Radio London listeners here at last was a DJ prepared to be a champion for the arcane and the esoteric, the unconsidered and the unlabelled.

Not everything John played would catch on with a wider audience, but a staggering amount did. Future Peel producer and Radio 1 Controller Trevor Dann, an early devotee of *The Perfumed Garden*, remembers queuing as a fifteen-year-old schoolboy for John's autograph. John was the rather rueful guest of honour at the opening of a summer garden party at a girls' school in rural Derbyshire, near where Dann lived. Meeting his hero, Dann later wrote, felt like 'meeting the Pope, or at least the Maharishi.'

As so many people would do over the next four decades, Dann recalled taping the shows, most memorably when Peel played the Beatles' *Sergeant Pepper* album the week it was released 'all the way through without speaking'. What DJ would do that now, let alone back then? John signed the youngster's copy of the fete programme – 'Love and Peace, John Peel' – but was dismissive when Dann proudly showed it to him years later, when they worked together at Radio 1. By now punk held sway and it was clear John did not welcome this unexpected reminder of a previous, less serious time. 'I used to talk a lot of bollocks in those days,' Dann reported John as saying.

Despite the deliberately 'hallucinogenic' overtones of his Radio London shows, John himself was no longer a regular drug user. 'I never even saw him smoke a joint,' the writer Germaine Greer later said. Once it dawned on him that he didn't *have* to do it, he said, he simply stopped. 'I was never a great one for drugs, really. I used to smoke dope in the sixties but it always used to make me feel slightly sick.' Once he'd rid himself of the somnambulism of the LSD and dope years, strong ale and vintage red wine would be the only drugs John would openly advocate, in person or on air (he always credited Rod Stewart and the Faces with reintroducing him to the pleasures of alcohol in the early seventies).

But then John's affinity with 'alternative' hippy culture had always stemmed more from his own stubbornly idealistic streak than from anything more ephemeral such as drugs. That and a devout love of the music were all he needed to connect with the new audience he was discovering on the *Perfumed Garden* shows. Broadcasting from a creaky stationary ship, anchored in the North Sea close to Felixstowe – just a few miles, coincidentally, from where he would later live with his second wife, Sheila – John viewed the hot, sunny months he spent on board the vessel as 'a bit of a holiday, really.'

The holiday came to an abrupt end, however, when, in August that year, Harold Wilson's Labour government passed the Marine Offences Act, thereby making all pirate stations illegal at a stroke. Although

Radio Caroline struggled on defiantly for a while (and continues to exist today in more conventional, fully legislated format on the internet), Radio London was one of the first to throw in the towel. Overnight, John and all the other DJs and backroom staff were made redundant – without the benefit of redundancy pay. 'They weren't called pirates for nothing,' as fellow Radio London DJ Tommy Vance later remarked to me.

Fortune smiled again, however, when word went out that the BBC were recruiting DJs in order to help produce their own version of the pirate stations – the first national pop station, to be named Radio 1. Launched in September 1967 – Tony Blackburn, the original breakfast show presenter, famously kicking off the whole shebang with 'Flowers in the Rain' by The Move – Radio 1 was to become John Peel's broadcast home for the next thirty-seven years. But at the time, he said, he thought he'd be lucky to last a year.

A session with an incoming controller of Radio 1 a year or so later is revealing of Peel's early position at Radio 1. Tellingly, John had been virtually the last to be interviewed as the controller worked his way through the DJs. Encountering a typically bluff BBC mandarin seated behind an unfeasibly large desk who regarded him with barely disguised contempt, John nearly walked out before the exchange had even started. Then, as he later recalled to author Simon Garfield, when it came up that John had been to public school, the old duffer brightened. 'Extraordinary! Which one?' When John said 'Shrewsbury' he almost exploded with delight. 'Good heavens! Which house were you in?' John told him and he became even more animated. 'How's old Brookie?' he asked. 'It was clear,' John said, 'that he thought, whatever he looks like, and whatever sort of unspeakable music he plays on the radio, he is still one of *us*. I think for a long time it was this factor that sustained me at the BBC ...'

Part of the now-famous group shot taken outside the station's original headquarters at Egton House, just off Regent Street, of the twenty-two founding presenters in the photograph – including such icons of pop grooviness as Bob Holness and Pete Murray – Peel is the only one not grinning inanely at the camera, looking almost disconsolate, in fact, as he gazes off away from the group somewhere into the distance.

After a laughable period of 'training' in BBC radio ways, John Peel began co-presenting *Top Gear* with Pete Drummond, amongst others. Operating initially under a short-term, six-week contract, Peel grew in popularity quickly enough to come a respectable seventh in a *Daily Mail* poll of Radio 1 DJs conducted shortly after the show first began airing. His contract was extended to three months. In February 1968 he became the sole presenter of *Top Gear* – at the prompting of Bernie Andrew, his first producer, who had been a big *Perfumed Garden* fan, and to the great consternation of

Andrew's superiors, who he said 'went stark raving mad!' when they found out.

Top Gear, according to the press announcement, was a show that would 'look at the outskirts of rock music'. Somewhat mystifyingly then, John's first live guest on the show was Lulu. Soon, however, the programme would forge a reputation, as *The Perfumed Garden* had before, for playing only the best from the new underground music scene, as exemplified by the music of new, experimental rock artists like King Crimson, Bolan, Bowie, Family, Fairport Convention, Jimi Hendrix, Arthur Brown, the Soft Machine, and Country Joe & the Fish — artists that seemed as mysterious and exotic to British listeners as the Beatles had a few years before to American fans. There were countless less well remembered artists regularly featured, too, like Ron Geesin and John Fahey — all interspersed with classic blues and folk music, book readings and a generally non-gravitational sense of humour. Displaying a consistently haughty attitude to whatever was in the Top Ten, John declared he was more interested in the stuff that wasn't in the charts than what was. Over the next four decades it would become his rallying cry.

Right from the outset, Peel changed the rules at Radio 1, insisting on playing the records without interruption, as he had at Radio London, while providing a wry but knowledgeable commentary. As such, *Top Gear* and the subsequent shows Peel would front – including the *Sounds of the Seventies*, which he was asked to present when *Top Gear* ended in 1969, and *In Concert* – would become the portal through which a nation of new British music lovers could access what was going on at a time when there were literally no other outlets for such sounds, such ideas.

The difference between the Radio 1 that John Peel joined in 1967 and the one he would leave behind thirty-seven years later was enormous. Still strictly limited by the amount of needle-time their shows were allotted – twenty minutes of music per hour being the maximum by law back then for a normal show – and with no ad breaks to fall back on, instead of simply back-announcing the records and keeping the hits coming, the first wave of Radio 1 DJs were encouraged to spiel endless inanities, not just to prove how 'groovy' and 'far out' they were, but in order to fill dead air.

One way of getting round the problem was to have other artists rerecord the hits of the day, for which the BBC could legitimately pay the musicians the same set rate as if they'd come into the studios and recorded a session, instead of the mounting royalties required by repeatedly spinning the original records. This would produce some bizarre, if unintentionally amusing recordings, such as the Northern Dance Orchestra sawing away prosaically at Hendrix's 'Purple Haze', which John later claimed he 'should love to have a copy of ... just unbelievable, really.'

Peel's own unique solution was to initiate the idea of broadcasting live sessions. Necessity being the mother of invention, this proved to be a master stroke. Recording live sessions also meant John needn't restrict his choices simply to major artists, and the idea of having new, unsigned acts doing sessions for *Top Gear* was introduced. Sometimes John would even coax different combinations of musicians together for a one-off 'jam' especially for the programme. Nobody was obliged to perform their singles or even any of the tracks from their current albums; bands could play anything they fancied on the night. John later said he saw it as 'an opportunity to actually advance the music a little bit, which is what we did.'

Occasionally, the music he broadcast caused raised eyebrows amongst the BBC hierarchy. As with Radio London, fortunately, evening radio was not high on the agenda for most senior BBC officials. Too busy congratulating themselves on the success of the station's anodyne but hugely successful daytime output, there were occasions, John later observed, when senior management 'seemed rather surprised that I walked upright and used knives and forks.'

John clearly despised most of his fellow, more conventional Radio 1 DJs, whose poptastic gibbering he openly derided on air – epitomised by Tony Blackburn, who he would mercilessly lampoon in his weekly column for *Sounds* magazine in the seventies. John Walters, who had taken over from Bernie Andrew as Peel's producer, fought his corner behind the scenes and for the most part the BBC was sensible enough to realise that it was Peel's perceived refusal to toe the line that was largely responsible for his popularity.

As Simon Garfield revealed in his book *The Nation's Favourite* – an in-depth study of Radio 1 in the mid-90s – the original BBC mandarins that hired Peel were 'old-style BBC through and through. They only hired him because he had worked in America and they thought that rang the right kind of bells. But they couldn't stand him and they didn't understand his show. John always said that he believed his survival was largely due to his late evening slot, at a time when most of them would have been at their gentlemen's clubs.'

When the Controller of Radio 1 once told Peel to stop playing Marc Bolan's records as he sounded like Larry the Lamb, John simply refused and continued to support his elfin-like friend as much as he could. As well as being the only DJ to actually play his early records, John also compered several university shows with Tyrannosaurus Rex and even personally introduced them onto the stage at the Isle of Wight Festival. Unlike the more guarded, distant stance he would assume over the last twenty years of his life – once claiming the nearest he'd got to being 'pally' with Mark E. Smith of the Fall, one of John's favourite bands, was 'a manly pat on the back' – in the late sixties John still saw himself as a friend to the musicians whose work he tirelessly promoted. In 1969, he volunteered to chauffeur his hero, Captain Beefheart, around the Midlands gig circuit on his UK tour. At one point, the good Captain ordered him to stop the car. 'John, I want to hug a tree!' he announced. John duly obliged.

John's reputation at the BBC as a loose cannon was hardly helped when, guest-hosting the evening discussion show *Night Ride*, he admitted that he had once been to a VD clinic, going so far as to describe the procedure. The Broadcasting House switchboard was jammed by angry calls from listeners and outraged parents. It caused such outrage, in fact, that the BBC was actually forced to draft a letter of apology to the Prime Minister. Within months, however, John was back hosting another discussion programme, *Inquiry*, on Radio 4.

In 1969, after trying his hand as producer for a group called the Liverpool Scene, John decided it would be 'fun' to form his own record label. Naming it Dandelion (after a favourite pet hamster), John and his new business manager, Clive Selwood, started the label together with the intention of trying to create a London-based equivalent of America's legendary Elektra Records (home to such groundbreaking artists as the Doors and Iggy and the Stooges). Over the next three years, Dandelion managed to put out over two dozen albums 'using other people's money'. As ever, John's talent-spotting ability was eclectic but – as he once described one of his first signings, Kevin Ayers – 'acute enough to perform major eye surgery with.' Amongst the dozens of almost wilfully uncommercial artists he signed, Clifford T. Ward, Bridget St John, Tractor, Mike Hart and a down-at-heel Gene Vincent were just the icing on a very weird cake. Then there was the obliquely named Principal Edward's Magic Theatre (a dozen art students from Bristol and Exeter, who he put up at his house for a time), Stackwaddy and Medicine Head – the latter having the distinction of giving Dandelion its solitary Top Thirty hit with 'Pictures in the Sky'.

Such a cavalier approach to commercial success could not last, of course. With John understandably forbidden from playing any of his own Dandelion releases on his Radio 1 shows, the core audience for such music was, ironically, deprived of its main chance of hearing any of it on the radio and the label would close in 1972 with considerable debts. That said, the twenty-six albums Dandelion released in the three years of its existence are all now regarded, in a very Peel-esque way, as collectors' items.

'It was just one of those things that seemed like a good idea at the time,' John later grumbled. At one point he even had the bizarre idea of forming a group called 101 Sharons – comprising 101 female singers named Sharon. Legend has it that he only finally abandoned the project when he reached forty. John also looked back with particular enthusiasm at one of the last groups he signed, Stackwaddy, whose album *Bugger Off* was actually played on Radio 1 by Annie Nightingale. 'They were punks before there were punks,' John would later explain. They were certainly something. When Stackwaddy toured America, the singer, a deserter from the US army, wore a wig everywhere to disguise himself. Then at their first gig he was so drunk he began by staggering to the edge of the stage and urinating on the unfortunate students gathered below. He was arrested shortly afterwards and the rest of the tour was cancelled.

As well as musicians and writers, John also met and encouraged a number of new young DJs. Bob Harris was one such beneficiary. Harris, who would later become famous for presenting *The Old Grey Whistle Test* – Britain's only 'serious' album-orientated TV programme in the seventies – had become hooked as a teenager on *The Perfumed Garden*.

'John was always the champion of everything new and innovative,' he later said. 'Back then he had just got back from America with a huge wodge of brand new vinyl albums by bands which back then no one had ever heard of in Britain, like the Steve Miller Band and Quicksilver Messenger Service. His philosophy was that the most important records in his collection were the ones that had arrived this morning, and he championed new music from when I first listened to him in 1967 right up to the present time.'

Apart from the unique mix of music, what made John's style of broadcasting so singular, Harris said, was that it felt as if there was 'virtually no gap' between the way John was in person and the way he was behind a microphone. 'With John, what you heard was what he was. He was erudite, he had a quirky way of looking at things, and he was extremely open in expressing his emotions, not just about music but about [everything].'

They had first met at the end of the sixties, when Bob came to interview John for his student paper. After a couple of hours, as Bob was leaving, John gave him an album and said, 'Here, take this with you, Bob. I think you'll really enjoy it.' It was Love's *Forever Changes*. A lovely story which Harris would tell again, nearly forty years later, on his Friday night Radio 2 show the week John's death was announced. Harris then rather movingly played a track from the album, 'Alone Again or?', before segueing into an early Tyrannosaurus Rex track, 'By the Light of the Magical Moon' from *Beard of Stars*.

Encouraged by John's patronage, Bob had actually made his first appearance on Radio 1, on 19 August 1970, sitting in for a holidaying John. Bob said he last saw him a few weeks before his death, bumping into him in the corridor outside the *Home Truths* office.

'Allo, young Bob,' John greeted him, as he always had since first meeting him as a student all those years before. Bob recalled how John was moaning that he kept getting stopped for his autograph by well-meaning but clearly misguided souls thinking he was Bob. (A story, in true Peel style, that may or may not have been true, but it certainly cheered Bob up, as was no doubt John's intention.)

Despite the wavering fortunes of his 'part-time record label', by the end of the 1960s, with Radio 1 at the very height of its popularity, John Peel was Britain's most famous and influential night-time DJ. He merely had to show an interest in a new band to draw the attention of managers, writers and record company executives. They may not always have followed his recommendations but those that did rarely had cause to regret it. As was the case with Doug Smith, a twenty-five-year-old, self-confessed 'former RAF brat' who, in the summer of 1969, was fronting a ramshackle, Ladbroke Grove-based management company called Clearwater.

'We were the same age as the bands and it was very eleventh-hour management, very chaotic,' Doug recalls. 'The only other company that was in touch with the new sort of psychedelic groups was Blackhill, who were managing the Floyd and also later took an office in Notting Hill.'

Every Friday, Clearwater put on a showcase for new

talent at the nearby All Saints Hall – an event which Peel would sometimes attend. Fortunately for Doug, John was there one Friday night in late August when, as he recalls, 'suddenly this bunch of complete freaks walked in the door out of their boxes, and said, "Here, we're a band, can we play for free?" They hadn't thought of a name yet, they just called themselves Group X. So I said, "All right."

'It was this psychedelic club with strobes going, two-and-six entrance, no booze, just orange squash and sandwiches,' Doug continues. 'Then this bunch of stoned loonies came on and they just went crazy, you know. Like nothing you'd ever seen or heard before. You didn't know what to think. But John was there and he saw all this and afterwards he came up to me and said, "Douglas, sign 'em. They could be big." I thought, hmmm, if John Peel thinks this is happening, maybe we better get on board …'

He did and so began the story of Group X – or rather Hawkwind, as they finally became known not long afterwards. Six months later they were signed to United Artists for the princely sum of £400, and it was Peel, inevitably, who became the first – often only – DJ to play their demented space jams on national radio. (When, in the late seventies, Hawkwind bassist – and singer of 'Silver Machine', the band's only recognisable hit in 1972 – Lemmy left the group to form Motorhead, once again it was Peel, his interest in Hawkwind having long since fizzled out, who gave them their first exposure. As John Walters once remarked, John could 'spot the speck of gold in all the muck. He rarely got it wrong.'

Now earning the sort of money from doing college gigs that 'embarrassed' him, despite the practised shoulder-shrugging and self-effacement, John certainly knew how to spend his money when the fancy took him. As if in emulation of his father, he began his own more modest but equally eye-catching car collection. He had brought back an ultra-desirable 1963 Corvette from America, followed by another 1963 Impala. Now, in order to ferry himself around to college gigs, he bought a Bedford Dormobile. 'It was a summer of '67 kind of car,' he said, and he and some friends dutifully drove it across Europe.

Back home in his Regent's Park pad, John became known as an easy touch for any struggling musician down on their luck and in need of new amplifiers, new instruments, or even in one case a new van. A then unknown Rod Stewart and David Bowie were both regular visitors, and he was always happy to 'sub' them. 'It was, "Hi, man, can you give us fifty quid for the arts lab?" It was always for the arts lab – and like a complete dickhead I used to give it to 'em. And they'd go off to the Speakeasy and buy velvet trousers ...'

CHAPTER TWO

'Hello and Welcome ...'

John Peel's success on Radio 1 with first *Top Gear* and then the show that succeeded it in 1970, *Sounds of the Seventies*, along with his wonderfully understated, almost to the point of bumbling, occasional appearances compering the BBC2 *In Concert* series, broadcast live from the Saville Theatre in Soho, led to the offer of presenting his own eponymously titled Radio 1 show – the name 'John Peel' now considered well-known enough, even by staid BBC standards, to act as a guarantee of quality to a certain otherwise under-serviced audience. Filling the largely unfancied ten-till-midnight slot, the programme was broadcast four nights a week, Monday to Thursday, with Fridays off. Remarkably, it was a slot Peel was to occupy – with occasional 'irksome' aberrations when he was moved to weekends or had the number of shows cut from four to two – for another thirty years.

By 1975, the blueprint for the John Peel show was already well established. The programme even had its own new theme tune. John opted to open the show each night with the low-down, sardonic-sounding dum-de-dum-de-dum of Grinderswitch's 'Pickin' the Blues', a musical motif that would become imprinted on the minds of all his listeners for generations to come – John's own signature tune, in fact, whether anybody actually knew what they were listening to or not (and of course, true to style, hardly anybody did).

Grinderswitch were, in fact, a little-known American boogie band from a small farming town in the deep south called Warner Robbins, formed in 1973. 'Pickin' the Blues' was an instrumental from their second album, *Macon Tracks*, released in 1974, on the then new Capricorn label. The band would spend the next ten years touring with the Allman Brothers Band, the Marshall Tucker Band, the Charlie Daniels Band, Wet Willie and, yes, Lynyrd Skynyrd. Unlike all of the aforementioned, however, Grinderswitch never had even a sniff of a hit, their biggest claim to fame being that one of their songs was used as the theme music on the Peel show – a programme, ironically, they never even got to hear. They have, however, recently reformed and now have – inevitably – their own website, Grinderswitch.com. How typical of John, though, to plump for what must be one of the least famous rock bands of all time for the source of what was to become perhaps his show's best-known tune.

I couldn't swear that he said it every single time he opened one of his shows, but in my memory, stretching from adolescence to middle age, John always seemed to begin with the words: 'Hello and welcome to the John Peel show.' They would come straight after the slide guitar figure from 'Pickin' the Blues' kicked in, at which point John would announce the 'menu' for that night's show. The usual litany of strange and often unpronounceable artists' names would follow. Regular listeners could also take delight in trying to spot the occasional made-up name that John would sometimes trail just for fun. 'And tonight, the Flying Creamshots in session,' he memorably announced one night. (In that instance, he had apparently lifted the phrase from a Dutch porn mag.)

John once said that the 1970s were 'the only time [my] show was ever fashionable.' Then he added, as if in apology for so frivolous an admission: 'I didn't really like the experience, though.' He was that anomaly: a music radio DJ preoccupied chiefly with, uh, music. It was this quality that most endeared him to his listeners. What might be called his impartial partiality. His great reluctance to oversell himself or settle for whatever currently passed as the Next Big Thing. On the whole, DJs at the BBC were not encouraged to be 'interested' in music. Programme building – the key decisions over which tracks would be played and when – was not the province of DJs at the BBC, heaven forfend. No, that was strictly up to the programme producers. DJs were merely presenters, linkmen, professional verbal gurners who would be handed their playlists on their way into the studio. Most of the early DJs at Radio 1 were happy with this arrangement. Not, though, John Peel.

As a result, in the early to mid-seventies, the name John Peel continued to grow in stature as he doggedly stuck to his idiosyncratic music selections, introducing his listeners first to the new 'progressive' rock sounds that emerged in the early seventies, epitomised by classically influenced virtuosos like Yes and Genesis. He was also the first Radio 1 DJ to herald the arrival of glam rock, inspired by the new-found success of his friends Marc Bolan and David Bowie, but most especially by his 'slack-jawed amazement' at the first two Roxy Music albums (*Roxy Music* in 1972, and *For Your Pleasure* in 1973) during that never-to-be-repeated period when Brian Eno was still there to add his cerebral, otherworldly sound effects to singer Bryan Ferry's more self-consciously stylised approach. But then, as John observed, in retrospect, the mid-seventies was a 'fairly boring period' for music in many ways, with few really new acts coming through. Rod Stewart, Bowie, Bolan, Elton ... all had been around for years before adopting the glitter. Roxy Music were 'almost the only band during the first three or four years of the seventies' that John viewed as genuinely new and exciting.

Peel also introduced his ever-indulgent listeners in the early years of the show to avant-garde new German artists like Can, Tangerine Dream and Kraftwerk; plus the first ever sessions from Bob Marley & the Wailers and, until Rod Stewart began to believe his own press and split the band for a new life in Hollywood with the actress Britt Ekland, healthy, well-oiled dollops of his old muckers the Faces. When it came to the latter, in fact, it could be argued that Peel became almost blinkered in his views towards them. Even though I was a big Faces fan myself at the time, for all their fine moments – encapsulated in what is still their only well-known hit, 'Stay With Me', in 1971 – looking back now, it's difficult not to see them as a largely overrated, poor man's Rolling Stones. Stewart was notorious for keeping his best songs for his solo albums. 'Maggie May' and 'You Wear It Well', No. 1 hits for him in both Britain and America, would have fitted snugly onto any Faces album and thereby improved their artistic reputation immeasurably amongst sterner critics who didn't happen to be mates with the band.

John's love for them remained frustratingly blind, however. I even recall him enthusing on air about the band's notoriously dreadful 1974 live album, *Overture and Beginners*, which even I, as an equally ardent fan, could plainly discern was awful, mainly because the band sound so staggeringly sloppy. Therefore I was astonished to hear Peel describe the album on the show as little short of a masterpiece, before going on to play several tracks, adding at one point that 'the band play like angels' – an assertion that even the band, who all later rejected the album as 'an embarrassment', found laughable. When, years later, I mentioned it to keyboardist Ian McLagan, he just chuckled broadly and said, 'Peely must have been as drunk listening to it as we were playing it.'

But then John never pretended – or set out – to get it right every time. By 1974 he was also reviewing singles every week for *Sounds* magazine, but he never really set himself up as a critic. Ultimately, one of the reasons he became such an endearing personality to his listeners was that he remained, at heart, an irredeemable fan, the same shamelessly myopic music worshipper he had been since schooldays. It was his blind devotion to those artists he believed in that later caused him to broadcast more than twenty sessions by the Fall, one of the unloveliest, if unique, British bands in history. And it was his incorrigible fanaticism that led him to unwittingly become the first Radio 1 DJ to play the same record back to back twice – as he did in 1978 with the Undertones' 'Teenage Kicks'.

The one thing all the different artists that appeared on the first Peel shows had in common, and the theme that would become the backbone to all future Peel shows, was that they had begun from an unpromising starting point, so far removed from whatever currently passed for the mainstream that without Peel they would have had little or no hope of receiving airplay on what was still the UK's only national pop station. Whenever one of his young protégés did go on to mainstream success, Peel formed the habit of moving on, impatient to see who else was out there waiting to be discovered – a great many of whom, it would become clear as the years went by, had first got the idea of becoming musicians through growing up listening to Peel shows.

Simple-minded critics sometimes accused him of wilfully dropping artists from the show as soon as they became played by anybody else, but that was never true. In reply, John argued that there was simply no more exciting moment in an artist's career than when they first arrived, sometimes still only half-formed. When they had no one to help them and tell them how it should be done, how all the others did it so they must too. Put simply, he said, once they became famous 'they also become extremely dull in a lot of cases.' He also pointed to his experience with Bolan and others as a warning against what can happen to such 'friendships' when success did come along. He compared the role of the show to that of 'a youth team at a football club,' he said. 'They go into the first team and then by and large turn their backs on us.'

John had promised early on to listen to everything he was sent, and for a long time, years, in fact, he was able to keep that promise. By the early nineties, however, over two decades and more than an estimated 100,000 records and tapes later, he was forced to admit that 'even if I stayed up day and night listening to these things for the rest of my life, I'd still never have time now to listen to it all.' One good practice he was able to keep up, however, was his insistence on replying personally to every letter and postcard he was sent, or more often as not in later years, email. This was quite an accomplishment considering the dishevelled mess of the office Peel shared with his producer throughout the seventies, the redoubtable John Walters: a maze the size of a broom cupboard, spilling over with hundreds of records and tapes piled high in Leaning Tower-like columns that reached to the ceiling.

While Peel was always quite meticulous in his ways, cataloguing every record he received, planning the guests for his shows weeks in advance, Walters was reputedly the untidiest man at the BBC, an imposing, ale-loving, bearded bear of a man, the like of which would sadly die out with the advent of today's computerised, open-plan offices. Peel and their long-suffering secretary Sue (known to both Johns as 'Brian' for some inexplicably 'wacky' seventies reason) would try badgering Walters into clearing up the mess occasionally but of course he never did. During their daily meetings, Walters would sit as best he could behind his desk, partly obscured by the mountain of stuff piled high upon it, while John would perch on his upturned record case or simply sit cross-legged on the floor amidst the detritus of old music papers, discarded running orders and unread memos from the top brass.

There was simply no room for a second chair.

Apart from his Radio 1 shows and writing for *Sounds*, John worked the college circuit relentlessly, where his DJ-ing services were always in high demand. He also enjoyed compering CND concerts, several Reading festivals and numerous other gatherings and events, both in Britain and abroad. And he began, somewhat impishly, to make more regular appearances on BBC1's flagship weekly chart run-down show, *Top of the Pops*.

John had been a semi-regular presenter of *Top of the Pops* since the black-and-white days of the late sixties. Clearly uncomfortable with the format, forced to talk up records he didn't personally rate merely because they were in the charts – something he would never have countenanced on his Radio 1 show – back then he had simply introduced the acts and run down the charts with as straight a face as possible. Now, in the seventies, he began to develop an ever more wry persona each time he was booked on the show. It was an attitude encapsulated in that funny little dance he always finished off his links with, as if so overtaken with excitement over the new Boney M single, or whatever, he just had to dance. Jigging along to the music was virtually a contractual requirement for everyone who presented the show, as all Radio 1 DJs were obliged to do on a round-robin basis in those days. Except in John's case, rather than trying to look cool, he would embark on the sort of mock twist an inebriated aunt might attempt at her horrified grandson's eighteenth birthday party. It was, without doubt, the most subversive thing ever seen on the show. Mocking but affectionately so, knowing without rubbing it in – a style entirely in keeping with his own slow-burn personality. Indeed, with his already receding hairline, unfashionably bearded visage and visibly growing paunch, it's hard to think of a more inappropriate presenter for such a show.

Most DJs back then used their Radio 1 profiles, still enormous in the seventies, not to promote music especially, but to promote themselves and then use that fame to piggyback into even more lucrative areas of the business like television and, in some cases, even their own music-related companies. John Peel may have been perceived as a lot of different things to a great many different people over the course of his life and career, but nobody ever mistook him for a shrewd businessman – as ably demonstrated by the collapse of the ill-fated Dandelion Records venture.

Despite his welcome if infrequent appearances over the years on what he still sometimes referred to as 'the goggle-box', Peel never coveted a career in television. He certainly rejected any suggestions of a possible TV version of his radio show. For a start, 'I was entirely the wrong shape – more egg cup than hourglass.' There was also the tricky question of what becoming a well-known TV face would actually entail and the probable impact it would have on his family. John was already recognised on the street enough times each day to shudder at the prospect of becoming even more well-known. Fame was merely an unfortunate by-product of his show, he seemed to suggest, not an aim in itself. As such, he found himself virtually alone amongst all the other DJs at Egton House, who clearly relished the vast opportunities to cash in Radio 1 now afforded them.

Speaking on Radio 4's *Live Chat* programme in 2001, John recalled how he 'always used to feel rather sorry for the people who hung around the doors of Radio 1, hoping to get to meet Noel Edmonds or some other radio great. They always used to be described as anoraks, a term I always hated.' Partly due to the fact, he confessed, that he often sported a three-quarter-length, festival-and-college-proof anorak himself at the time. 'I always felt I was an anorak who managed to get into the inside,' he said.

But if it's true he never openly sought the big score, John did, however, continue to make the most of the 'silly money' he was offered to DJ at clubs and colleges – sometimes as much as £700 a night. Big money in the days when the average working man was earning less than a tenth of that a week. With his typically understatedly named 'John Peel Roadshow – A Man and a Box of Records', at one stage in the mid-seventies, John would do as many as three live gigs a week, driving from polytechnic to polytechnic each weekend in his newly purchased Land Rover-based camper, often sleeping in chilly lay-bys, surviving on sandwiches, cans of Coke and bags of chips. 'I was the king of the polytechnics,' he later claimed sardonically. After he moved out of London in the early eighties, the Land Rover also became a useful mobile dorm on those week nights when he was in London doing his Radio 1 shows.

On more than one occasion, John found himself booked to appear before several hundred rowdy students who were already out of it on cheap student union beer and whatever else they had been able to get their grant-assisted hands on. These were the crowds John hated playing to the most: the ones who never liked any of the records he fished from his box, almost on a point of principle, though more usually because John, bloody-minded as ever, would decide to punish them by playing the most obscure tunes from his collection. At which point the students would first try heckling him, even throwing glasses and bottles on occasion. When that didn't work, they would simply ignore him and resort to more familiar pastimes like beer-drinking competitions and games that involved wearing your trousers on your head.

'In my own defence,' John later recalled in the *Guardian*, 'I always warned the resentful students what to expect. "I'm going to play records you don't like very much for an hour or so," I told them. "Then I'm going to walk away with my pockets bulging with your money." This admittedly high-risk strategy usually paid off, although I twice had to be rescued from whatever is the opposite of fans by the police.'

In an effort to avoid the regular potential lynching he knew he faced in certain parts of the country, he admitted that at one point he even 'shockingly, employed go-go girls,' to try and make the show more popular with such crowds. 'I'm not sure what the current position is on go-go girls, but given that theoretically liberal people seem almost keen on lap-dancing and similar entertainments these days, I assume it's pretty relaxed,' he said. 'I can't, I'm afraid, remember the names of "my" go-go girls, but I do remember that they came from Luton. They accepted the work, I suspect, because they hoped that by dancing for the John Peel Roadshow they might get to meet Noel Edmonds or even Dave Lee Travis. Alas, as far as I know, this impossible dream remained just that. Sorry, girls.'

In what little spare time he had, John would also happily agree to put in an appearance at any number of less heralded, often unpaid events, such as the annual talent contest he agreed to judge for many years at Scunthorpe town hall and the charity events he would either donate prizes for or just turn up to. Johnny Green, who in the late seventies would become tour manager for the Clash, recalls writing to John at Radio

London when he was a schoolboy growing up in Gillingham.

'Where we were, you got a really good signal for all of the pirates but John's *Perfumed Garden* show was always my favourite,' he says. 'It was all Country Joe & the Fish and Captain Beefheart. It opened my ears right out ... Then one day, while listening to his show, I got the idea into my head of putting on my own little concert. I'd never been a muso but I'd helped out a lot of friends that had started bands and stuff like that, and so I thought I would put on this mini sort of outdoor festival in some fields nearby where I lived, featuring all these local groups I had some sort of connection with.

'I wrote to John asking him if he would broadcast the fact that I was doing this and when the date of the show was, and to my amazement he actually wrote back saying he would. He even agreed to come along himself, which was incredibly nice of him, considering it was only a kid with no connections whatsoever asking him for this favour.

'In the end, unfortunately, the council turned down the application I needed to hold the event and so it never happened. But again, John was incredibly sweet about it. He wrote back to me, offering encouragement and for a while we struck up a correspondence together. At one point he even sent me his address in London and invited me to come and visit him. I took him up on his offer but when I got there he wasn't home. This was when he still lived down in Fulham and I remember sitting on his doorstep, waiting for him to come home.

'Next thing, Marc Bolan turned up looking for John, too. This was still a few years before he became really famous but I knew who he was straight away because of all the times he'd been on Peel. He seemed like a lovely guy, too. We must have sat there together on the doorstep just chatting, waiting for John to come home, for about half an hour. Then we both gave up and went home. A few days later I got this incredibly nice letter from John, apologising for missing me.

'After that, we sort of lost touch, though, and I didn't see him again for a few years. By then I was living up north in a commune. One day I heard that John was doing one of his roadshows at York University, accompanied by the Third Ear Band, as I recall. So five of us all piled into this broken-down car we shared and headed off there to see if we could blag our way in. We didn't have enough money between us to afford to buy tickets, we just hoped we'd get in the back way.

'No matter what we tried, though, we couldn't get in. It was a drag. We were just about to start the long journey home again when I spotted John getting out of his car. Sensing this was our last chance, I went up to him, explained the situation, that we were poor hippies from a commune and didn't have the money for tickets, and asked him straight out if he could get us in. I didn't mention who I was or remind him that we had once written to each other; I just sort of put him on the spot.

'He took it all with his usual good grace, though. He explained that no, there wasn't really anything he could do on that score, that the university had its own rules and we had to respect that. Then he did something extraordinary which I've never seen anyone else in the music business do. He put his hand into his pocket and dug out some money and gave it to me – enough for five tickets. I couldn't believe it, the incredible generosity of the man, the human spirit. Just to dig in like that out of his own pocket for a bunch of freaks that, as far as he knew, he didn't even know.

'I never forgot that, it influenced my way of thinking as much as, if not more than, anything he ever played on his show. I took inspiration from that when I later worked with the Clash. I always used to go outside at every Clash gig and try and make sure that any stragglers that really didn't have the money to see the show but that I knew loved the band could get in. I used to take them round the back, through the roadies' entrance, or up and down fire escapes – anything just to get 'em in. The boys in the band knew I did it – Joe Strummer used to practically insist on it. For me, though, it all stemmed from that incident with Peel.'

Since leaving Shirley, John had lived alone in Regent's Park and had a number of girlfriends. That he may also have availed himself of the occasional groupie during this period is not something he would have denied. While still espousing the egalitarian ideals of the sixties, John saw no reason, as a single man again, not to indulge himself in some of the early seventies' more outré pursuits. Being interviewed by Joan Bakewell, in 2003, John even came out with the startling revelation that one of his many conquests in this period had been the feminist writer Germaine Greer. He had met Germaine between marriages, he said, and they had become friends. But then, he claimed, he became targeted by Greer during her 'sleeping with everyone famous' period. 'It just happened to be my night after George Best.' The experience, though, 'taught me a valuable lesson,' he went on. 'She was a friend, somebody I liked and admired, and then she decided to presume on a friendship and push it a step too far. I actually found myself saying, "Look, I like you too much, I don't want to do this." And she made me.' Greer, somewhat understandably, was appalled by this 'ungallant' public outing and responded by saying she didn't recall John putting up much of a fight.

'By the time I got to know John in the mid-seventies,' says Alan Lewis, Peel's editor at *Sounds* in the late seventies, 'he was clearly presenting himself as a bumbling incompetent as a way, partly, I suspect, to put others at their ease in his company. But you have to remember, he was already very successful by then. And although that self-deprecatory humour became his hallmark, I always felt that deep down John knew his true worth. He was also a slightly more exotic-looking figure back then than the avuncular sort of chap we came to know him as in later life. He still had quite long, dark hair, he was a good-looking guy, and it was clear he'd done his fair share of carousing in his younger years.'

All that came to an end, however, when, in 1974, John married for the second time. His bride, Sheila Mary Gilhooly, was the beautiful, dark-haired daughter of a northern mill worker. Then training to become a teacher, she had begun seeing John the year before, after he had spotted her in the audience during an outside broadcast he was making and duly sent her a note. John was thirty-five years old when they decided to wed; Sheila was twenty-five. John was 'never so happy before in my life'. On the occasion of his sixtieth birthday, he told a BBC TV documentary crew how, until then, he had tended to go for 'models who weren't really models and actresses that weren't really actresses.' John would pontificate in the more eccentric manner of his early shows and 'they would go, "Wow, John, that's really beautiful." But Sheila would say, "Oh, you daft pillock!"' At first, he mistook this for 'impertinence' before 'realising that it was true and that I was, in fact, a daft pillock.' Soon 'all the models and actresses had disappeared and there was only Sheila.'

Because of John's work commitments, they had honeymooned in Egypt – taking in the Pyramids, which John later described as 'one of the few sights I've seen that really exceeded my expectations', and accompanied by John Walters and his wife – before the actual wedding on 31 August. 'We got married the day after my birthday quite deliberately so I'd not forget,' he joked.

John famously nicknamed Sheila 'The Pig' – always referring to her as such on air and in the new John Peel column he had begun for *Sounds*. Not in any derogatory sense, but because of his delight in her snorting laugh, which he heard often as, remarkably, Sheila always seemed to find John's jokes even funnier than he did. Rod Stewart attended the wedding reception, and John later recalled with amusement looking across the room to see Rod in deep conversation with one of his aged, car-loving aunts. 'I would love to have known what they were talking about,' he said. Bugattis, perhaps?

At the register office wedding, both the bride and groom wore red and white in honour of John's beloved Liverpool Football Club. Sheila, whose indulgence of John's ways was seemingly endless, even agreed to let him have 'You'll Never Walk Alone' as the processional music. At the same time, John's love for his young wife knew no bounds. When Sheila crashed the new Renault 5 John had bought her as a wedding present – 'a wonderful car,' he later recalled – she was thankfully unhurt. Nevertheless, John waited until she was having a piano lesson and then filled the car with flowers.

Soon they had the first of what would eventually be two sons and two daughters – a boy, William, in 1976, followed at regular two-year intervals by Alexandra, Thomas and Florence. John remarked that he looked forward to 'vigorous parenting' and his young family now became the main focus in his life. Though all would bear the surname Ravenscroft, rather than Peel, John did manage to give all his children extra middle names that celebrated the football team. William and Alexandra both ended up with 'Anfield' (the name of Liverpool's ground); Thomas inherited 'Dalglish' (after Liverpool's most celebrated goal-scorer and John's favourite player of all time); Florence, or Flossie as she was always known to her dad, got 'Shankly' (after the legendary Liverpool manager who led the team from the Second Division to the top of the First and FA Cup success).

Joshing aside, more than anything, John and Sheila wanted to provide a solid family base for their young family, and by the start of the eighties they had moved out of London and into a rambling thatched farmhouse set in eight acres near Stowmarket, in Suffolk. Complete with swimming pool, tennis court and vegetable garden – by now both John and Sheila were vegetarians – this was the place that would famously become known as Peel Acres. Only the white 1963 Chevy almost guiltily concealed in the garage was left over from his younger, wilder days. Living in Suffolk meant he had to spend longer on the roads in his car, but John always enjoyed driving anyway. His preferred route to London was the A505 around Royston to the A1. Not as direct, perhaps, as the more popular A10 but that was John's way. It was just 'nicer'.

Sheila, meanwhile, became his new benchmark, he claimed, for what should be played on the show. If the Pig danced around the house to one of the records or tapes he was listening to, that meant it was good. If the Pig danced in the garden, however, it meant it was great! It was the early years of their love, of course, but John would remain just as passionately devoted to his wife throughout their thirty-year marriage. He even once confessed to 'making love to my wife during a long record whilst theoretically on air.'

Because of the humble, downbeat style he always projected in public, and with a new, more settled home life behind him, John seemed to be taking all his various responsibilities throughout this period very much in his stride. But the late nights and constant travelling were starting to catch up with him, even before he and Sheila moved out of London. To compensate, he took to having a late-afternoon nap every day. Usually, he would go home to Regent's Park for this or, later, after the move to Suffolk, he might retreat to his draughty camper. Sometimes, though, having returned at some ungodly hour the night before from the latest out-of-town college gig he had hosted (and pocketed another hefty fee for), John was so exhausted he would simply curl up on the floor of the cluttered production office, his body wrapped around the legs of Walters' desk.

Meanwhile, on the show each night he was busy perfecting what he called his 'anti-DJ' style – characterised by an almost pathological reserve as a presenter coupled to an utterly unyielding attitude to the music he played. Such was his reputation at this stage that if you had your record played by Peel or, better still, had a session broadcast on the show, it was regarded as the ultimate hallmark of quality – almost an end in itself for some groups.

The hippest record company A&R men began to listen in regularly. They didn't always go for whatever John was currently getting carried away about, but they trusted his ears more than anybody else's when it came to identifying the best of the new 'album-oriented' artists then breaking through, as album sales began to overtake those of singles for the first time. By the mid-seventies, albums – or LPs, as John always insisted on calling them – had become the chief proving ground for any artist worthy of more than cursory attention. It was a cultural shift that arguably reached its apotheosis when, in 1973, John elected to play both sides of *Tubular Bells*, the debut album by a then unknown Mike Oldfield.

John Peel with the newest addition to the Peel family, his grandson Archie, in April 2004. (*Amit Lennon, Camera Press*)

The late sixties and early seventies and 'the world is divided into two camps – Love and Hate, and Love will eventually win . . . Touch the bark of a thousand trees, shoeless . . . then go to the children's playground in Kensington Gardens and stare at the elves

on the trees there.' This was the sort of hydroponically charged
space talk that would cause John Peel a mixture of amusement and
regret whenever reminded of it in later life.
(*All Rex Features, far right, Peter Sanders*)

The 'stellar' Radio 1 line-up through the ages: 1967, '77 and the '97 reunion. Peel, of course, outlasted them all.
(*All BBC; 1997, Tim Anderson*)

1997

John, in seasonal high spirits, at the Radio 1 Christmas party, 1980. (*PA*)

Gene Vincent, Duane Eddy, Clyde McPhatter and Eddie Cochran all heralded the arrival of rock and roll and 'the teenager', and, as such, all had a great impact upon the young John Ravenscroft. (*Brian Moody/Rex Features*)

The conscientious young DJ at work. (*Dave Pickthorn/BBC*)

Introducing Tyrannosaurus Rex on stage at the Isle of Wight
Festival, 1970. (*John Selby/Rex Features*)

The 'models who weren't really models and actresses who weren't really actresses' soon drifted away and 'there was only Sheila'. John and Sheila's wedding outfits are in red and white – Liverpool colours. (*Michael Putlang/Retna*)

A bravura, symphony-length, instrumental album consisting of ever more elaborate variations on its central theme, a haunting refrain tiptoed out on an electronically treated keyboard – primitive by modern digitally enhanced standards, but utterly innovative in its day – *Tubular Bells* would, of course, go on to become one of the mightiest oaks ever to have sprung from one of Peel's little acorns. It has since sold squillions of copies, laying siege to the charts in both Britain and America (where it became famous after being used to astonishingly powerful effect as the eerie soundtrack for the 1974 horror film *The Exorcist*) throughout the rest of the decade. The boost this also gave Branson's fledgling Virgin Records cannot be underestimated, either. In fact, it's unlikely there would have been a Virgin Records as we know it now, had Peel not bucked trends, as usual, and got behind *Tubular Bells*, which was the first and until then only planned release on Virgin, a hastily put-together independent – in what would become the finest Peel tradition – formed by Branson with the last of the overeager ex-public schoolboy's savings when no other label would release it. Oldfield had recorded it all at his own home-studio (another prophetic echo of future Peel favourites).

As Alan Lewis says now, John's role as the chief talent-broker for numerous new artists who wouldn't otherwise have stood a chance of being played on national radio, let alone signed to a major record company, 'cannot be overstated – his influence all the stronger for plainly coming from an entirely non-biased, non-commercial standpoint.'

Nevertheless, in weaker moments, usually when his six-monthly contract was coming up for renewal, John would confess to friends that he still half expected to be sacked any week, sitting there gloomily over a glass of red, considering his limited future employment prospects. In the early days, according to Radio 1 folklore, John felt so insecure about his position that on one occasion when he was ordered to take a holiday by Walters, he instead chose to turn up at the station just to stare at his stand-in. The stand-in in question, Mark Ellen, wrote in *Word* magazine how 'fifteen minutes into [his third] show, I felt a presence in the control room. Through the glass, the unmistakable silhouette of Peel.'

However, despite his occasional lapse into paranoia, the John Peel show was now bigger and more popular than ever. Many of John's friends from the sixties were also now famous. By 1971, Marc Bolan had gone electric, shortened the group's name to the easier-to-say T. Rex, and begun a rollercoaster ride up the charts with twelve consecutive hit singles over the next three years, beginning with a trio of some of the greatest hits of the era – 'Ride A White Swan' in October 1970, 'Hot Love' in February 1971 and 'Get It On' in July 1971 – and concluding with 'The Groover', the last T. Rex single to reach the UK Top Ten, in June 1973.

Having stood by Bolan through thin and thinner in the years preceding his new-found success, ironically, now that the good times were finally rolling for both of them, the two fell out. Unlike Rod and the Faces, who still sent John regular postcards from wherever they were on tour in the world and made a point of staying in touch, Bolan used his leapfrogging success to distance himself from Peel. Why? According to Bolan, who had led a chequered career that involved the patronage of several 'well-wishers', male and female, before hitting the big time, and was known for his 'selective' memory about those days, the reason they stopped being friends was that 'John Peel thought we had sold out.'

Speaking in 1976, he added incongruously: 'I can see now that he was helping himself more than us. He needed an obscure group he could use and we were that group. He didn't like "Ride A White Swan" at all and he was paranoid that we would do anything that was even remotely commercial. I haven't seen him since and he certainly never plays our records now.'

In fact, John had adored 'Ride A White Swan'. It was the follow-up, 'Hot Love', which he had refused to play, simply because, he said, 'I didn't like it.' By then Marc was already refusing to take his calls. John later remembered phoning on a number of occasions only to be met with a curt 'Marc's busy, he'll call you back' –

except, of course, he never did. After a while, John simply 'took the hint' and stopped phoning.

It was strange; John didn't understand it. Until then, he had considered Marc and his wife June his 'best mates'. They had hung out together for years, they went to gigs and parties together, drank and smoked dope and dreamed of better times together. In the early days, whenever John was booked to do a college gig, he would drag Marc along with him, long before anyone had ever heard of him. John happened to be driving to another such gig one afternoon in November 1970 when he heard the news on his car radio that 'Ride A White Swan' had gone to No. 1. He was so overcome with emotion, he said, he had to pull over into the nearest lay-by and 'have a little cry'.

They were 'very good pals,' John later told the *Guardian*. 'But it was like with a lot of one's friends, there's another side to them, because we all have darker sides which we try to suppress. I suppose a way that one measures people as human beings is by their ability to suppress the disagreeable things which might bubble up. I always knew about Marc that he was very ambitious, but then from the moment he became a real star, we were just cut off like that, which was just upsetting really. I saw him once more before he died.'

As glam rock fell out of favour, Bolan failed to find a way to move on, unlike contemporaries such as Bowie and Ferry. His career began to slide and by the mid-seventies, despite experimenting with a funkier sound in an effort to stay relevant, the hits had dried up. When Marc died in a car crash on Barnes Common, driving home from a recording session with his live-in partner, singer Gloria Jones, in September 1977, John was 'greatly saddened' by the news. But he did not attend the funeral at Golders Green Crematorium.

Charles Shaar Murray, then one of the star writers on the *NME*, once recalled how 'meeting [John] in the 1970s was a delight. He was just as cool, wise, sardonic and self-deprecating as he seemed on radio, even retaining good humour when he overnighted at my flat and got his feet sprayed by my un-neutered tomcat.' By 1976, however, it could be argued that the Peel show's influence was starting to wane a little as the music he had been responsible for popularising became increasingly mainstream. A new generation of Radio 1 DJs like Bob Harris and Annie Nightingale had also come along and begun presenting evening shows that covered similar territory: Little Feat, Van Morrison, the Eagles ... Even though John was still the only one likely to play Bob Marley & the Wailers back to back with the Flamin' Groovies, as he later said of the period, 'You didn't realise you were being bored until you stopped being bored.'

Then came punk. If Peel had tried the patience of out-of-touch BBC controllers with his previous blend of hippy mysticism and inscrutably obscure music, his new taste for punk left them dumbfounded. They had never understood the music Peel played on his shows, but at least it had seemed relatively harmless. Punk was something else. Following the fracas over the Sex Pistols' expletive-infused appearance on early-evening TV with Bill Grundy, punk was downright objectionable. Worse still, it seemed to offer some actual threat to the status quo – and not just the group of the same name.

With British music clearly about to undergo its most vibrant and exciting period since the late sixties, John was determined not to get left behind and that the show should nail its new colours defiantly to its mast for all to see. When, in the summer of 1976, punk rock began to erupt across the music scene like an angry red boil, John was the first Radio 1 DJ to play its earliest, most influential releases.

John later admitted that, at first, he had been as taken aback by the arrival of the first punk records as everybody else of his generation clearly was. There had definitely been 'a few weeks of adjustment' he'd had to make. But he decided, in the end, that enough people who listened to his show would agree with him and welcome the invigorating approach punk engendered. He really did think, rather naively, he later admitted, that people would throw away their old Bob Dylan and Stones albums and start listening to the Pistols and the Damned instead. Discovering the Ramones for the first time, as he had done that summer when they released their first self-titled album in April 1976, was no different, he suggested, from when he first heard the original rock'n'roll of the fifties. Listening to 'New Rose' by the Damned – the first ever recognisably punk single on Stiff Records, the first new independent punk label – gave him exactly the same feeling as the first time he ever heard Little Richard.

As a result, overnight, it seemed, the playlist of the Peel show switched from the Steve Miller Band to Siouxsie and the Banshees; from well-crafted mid-seventies somnambulance to the home-made spit and fury of new, worryingly named groups like the Sex Pistols, the Clash, the Stranglers and the Damned. (The mother of the Damned's unfortunately named drummer, Rat Scabies – real name: Chris Miller – later wrote John a lovely letter after he had given the band their first session on the show, thanking him sincerely for 'helping Christopher with his career'.)

The risk Peel took in doing so is often underestimated now. With practically no support whatsoever from anyone at the BBC, bar the eternally supportive if still somewhat baffled Walters, John also succeeded in alienating much of his long-standing audience, a vast number of whom now switched their Radio 1 allegiance to Bob Harris, who was still playing the rock 'supergroups' that the punks now publicly ridiculed as – in the words of Pistols singer Johnny

Rotten – 'dinosaurs' and 'boring old farts'.

Peel's early, wholesale adoption of what was swiftly dubbed the 'new wave' divided his regular listeners like nothing he had ever played before. He even began to receive abusive, threatening mail, yet he continued to plug away, playing the things he thought he should. But if the Peel show tottered for a few crucial weeks, the slack was soon taken up by an enormous influx of new, mainly younger listeners – an entire new audience, in fact, who, like previous generations, admired the fact that he was playing music no other DJ would even consider at that time. When the Sex Pistols released their first single, 'Anarchy in the UK', in November 1976, it caused such uproar – including several objections from stars of the day like Steve Harley – that EMI withdrew it from general sale less than two weeks later. When they did, Peel made a point of playing it so anyone who hadn't had the chance to purchase it in the brief time it was available could tape it.

However, the Peel show pointedly declined to offer the Sex Pistols a session. John wanted to but Walters had blocked the move after attending the infamous show at the 100 Club in the summer of 1976 at which the Pistols were supported by the Clash, and practically everyone who later became someone in punk was there to see it – from Sid Vicious and Siouxsie Sioux to Don Letts, Julian Temple and many others. A former art teacher, Walters later claimed he could see the Pistols 'had something' but that the singer 'didn't look like the sort of boy you chose to hand out the scissors.' Peel would continue to badger Walters about booking a Pistols session but, in the wake of first the uproar over the band's teatime appearance on ITV with Bill Grundy, and their subsequent dropping like a hot potato by first EMI and then A&M, Walters smelled trouble and didn't trust the band 'alone in a BBC studio with only some poor engineer to cope with them.' Fair-minded to the end, the producer later admitted it was 'my one big regret about that time. We should have booked them...'

As if to make up for this profligacy, Peel became the only Radio 1 DJ to defy the 'unofficial' ban the BBC had placed on the second Pistols single, 'God Save the Queen', and play it in its uninhibited entirety on his show when it was finally released on Virgin in May 1977. Not bad for someone who was threatened with a beating the one and only time he encountered Sid Vicious at a gig. Released in time to go to straight to No. 1 the same week the entire country was supposed to be celebrating the Queen's Silver Jubilee, this was viewed by the BBC as a shocking confluence of the stars. 'More embarrassing than shocking, actually,' says one former Radio 1 executive from those days. Something the BBC allegedly moved to rectify swiftly by slyly swapping the chart position of 'God Save the Queen' with the single at No. 2 that week, the more acceptably saccharine Rod Stewart ballad 'The First Cut is the

Deepest' for that week's chart run-downs on both Radio 1 and *Top of the Pops*.

This, to Peel, amounted to downright discrimination, and he redoubled his efforts to focus the show more on punk and the various, often more intriguing, new-wave offshoots it was now producing. For the first time since *The Perfumed Garden*, he had become almost evangelical about music again, complaining in the *NME* of the nameless Radio 1 producer who wouldn't even consider playing any single that arrived in a picture sleeve, as that meant it was punk and he had already made up his mind that he didn't like punk, almost on a point of principle. To get round the problem, John said, record pluggers from indie labels were now putting their pre-release records into plain white sleeves in the vain hope that the producer might actually listen to a few seconds of it.

Even on those rare occasions when one of the daytime-show producers would actually express an interest in something as innocuous as Generation X, he was knocked back, John said. 'The reaction would be, "No, mate, sniff, it's punk innit – I've got kids." How can you compete with that? And then you try and talk to them about the sociological, let alone the political, aspects of what's going on, and you can't even get to first base. If you can't kiss them, you can't expect to spend the night with them. It's an impossible task, really.'

But if most mainstream pundits initially shunned punk as a particularly unpleasant fad, there were soon just as many others out there who were following developments on the Peel show with more than a passing interest again. Alan Lewis confesses that he used to base a great deal of the editorial policy at *Sounds* in the late seventies around what John was currently playing on his show.

Alan Lewis: 'With the emergence of punk in 1976, just like Peely, I decided we should jump in with both feet at *Sounds*. John was very much part of that, of course. I certainly used to come in next day and say, "Why haven't we done anything on ...?" It wasn't just that Peel's show was essential listening. I've always felt that journalists don't listen to the radio enough. They're either out at gigs or being schmoozed by PRs and often miss out on what Joe Public is hearing. Probably less true now, but I always felt back then that with a weekly it was your duty to react quickly to what the punters were hearing.

'Obviously we had a good young team with their ears to the ground, but by tapping into what Peel was doing as well it meant we didn't miss a thing – and it helped *Sounds* come from the bottom of the pile in '76 to become the biggest-selling weekly by '79. We just reacted really quickly and did the very first features on most of the punk/new wave bands. Meanwhile *NME* and the *Melody Maker*, with their more established reputations, tended to hang back, and that gave us the opening we needed.

'Peel definitely helped to keep us on our toes. The classic example was when he played "New Rose" by the Damned for the first time. We had already done a feature on the band for next week's issue but the cover story was due to be an exclusive interview with Rod Stewart. At that time *Sounds* was already doing a lot of stuff on the new pub-rock/proto-punk bands, but Rod was still seen as a "cover star". We had more or less put the issue to bed, but that night driving home I heard Peel give the first ever play to "New Rose", which was actually the first UK punk single. It sounded so great that it was a sort of epiphany. I went in next day and pulled the Rod Stewart cover and put the Damned on instead. We never looked back after that ...'

Sounds also rode on the coat-tails of the Peel show's success by giving him his own weekly column to write. 'We certainly understood the value of having John attached to the paper,' says Lewis, 'splashing his name on the cover each week. When he gave up reviewing the singles, we didn't want to lose him so we more or less gave him a free hand to write whatever he liked, hence the John Peel Column.

'John's column was one of the best things about the mag. We had some research done which showed that most readers turned to his column first each week. His copy was always absolutely immaculate, too:

punctuation, grammar, spelling – everything spot on. And of course the writing was wonderfully erudite. We used to get it and put it straight into the magazine.'

Lewis also commissioned a special photo session for John 'so that we would have something more interesting to run with his column than the usual mug-shot. Because John was quite fond of mentioning schoolgirls in it and suchlike, it was arranged for some suitably scantily clad models to join in the session with him. For years afterwards, we always ran a picture of John standing or sitting there looking quite unobtrusive, except with this naked, or semi-naked, young woman standing somewhere in the background. You have to remember, this was the seventies and such things were still considered amusing, even clever. And for some reason we all felt it suited his column perfectly. We got mileage out of those pictures for years. By today's standards, it was amazingly politically incorrect, but if you understood John's humour, it seemed to work – and of course it helped draw readers to his column.'

The references to schoolgirls in the columns, says Lewis, 'were always sort of half-joking, half-serious. The fantasy of the sexually aware teenage schoolgirl is an iconic one – hence things like those School Disco events that are so popular today – and in that respect John was no different to any other man. But we really did go quite far, on occasion. One picture we used

endlessly was of John surrounded by assorted
schoolgirls in St Trinian's mode, short gym skirts,
stockings and suspenders and so forth. We even ran one
of him in the bath with them! It sounds disgraceful but
it did look quite funny and incongruous.'

Ultimately, maintains Lewis, 'John was sending
himself up. A great deal of his column also talked about
life at Peel Acres with the Pig etc. He made it clear
that he was, in fact, quite domesticated, and that most
of his relationships with women were bumblingly
unsuccessful. He was also married by then and was the
father of two small children. I had a couple of very
young children of my own at the time and I remember
how happy he was to chat about them whenever we
went for a drink together. It was never all just about
music with John, even though music clearly came
pretty close to top of the list.

'John used to come up to the office to drop his
copy off and we would go to the pub together
sometimes for lunch. I remember one occasion where
John and I were joined in the pub by the mag's
cartoonist, Alan Moore, who later became a very
famous graphic-novel writer with his *Watchmen* series,
and then *Sounds* writer Garry Bushell, who also went
on to find his own kind of fame, of course. John
wouldn't stay that long, just for a couple of drinks, but
he could chat to anyone on any level. Then he'd be on
his way to the Beeb, where he and Walters would spend

the afternoon sorting through records, preparing his show.'

Lewis would go back to the *Sounds* office where he would read the column for the first time – laughing out loud. 'A typical example might comprise some wry comment about a band he'd recently seen, or a DJ-ing gig he'd done, always playing it down, you know, the "grumpy fat man spinning records" who claimed to be embarrassed by how much he was paid. Then he might slip in a comic bit about Walters or some surreal tale involving the Pig.

'He would have various pet themes, too. Like his general contempt for Tony Blackburn, who epitomised the sort of gibbering Radio 1 DJ John was the antithesis of. John always used to refer to him in the column as Timmy Bannockburn.' Indeed, John admitted years later that back then he really did see Blackburn as 'the Antichrist'. He added with a snort: 'We were told he was the most important man in British broadcasting and we must treat him with utmost respect.'

Lewis also recalls how 'when all else failed he used to inject "excerpts" from what he claimed was his forthcoming novel, *Buckskins & Buggery: A Tale of the Old West*. Right in the middle of the column you might suddenly get 500 words of this, admittedly amusing, nonsense. I didn't know then that John had been to public school, and quite a posh one at that, but it quickly became apparent that he was obviously well read. He'd obviously absorbed a lot from an earlier generation – these sort of Edwardian boys' own adventure pastiches he perfected long before Michael Palin made *Ripping Yarns*. John had clearly imbibed a lot of H. Rider Haggard and G.A. Henty, gung-ho stories full of tousle-haired heroes and marvellous tales of derring-do. He'd obviously read a lot of P.G. Wodehouse, too, which he'd slip quite a lot of into the column too.'

The other intriguing development punk made that John strongly approved of was the shift in emphasis away from albums and back towards singles. He realised, he said, that he preferred the music of what he called 'primitives': artists – like the early Elvis and Gene Vincent – who specialised in a form of music that was basic, direct and done quickly, warts and all. Indeed, it was the 'warts and all' that John often found most intriguing.

His biggest problem since punk had first stormed the show, he said, was the mountainous number of demo tapes he was now sent. Inspired by punk's do-it-yourself ethos, everyone was suddenly forming a band, it seemed. By the end of the seventies, he was getting sent up to a dozen a day, and had built up a backlog of over five hundred unheard demo tapes. For the first time, John struggled to keep his promise about listening to everything he was sent, not that that stopped him trying, and he would often find himself 'spending eight hours a day, every day, just listening to music.'

Before punk, the Peel show could usually expect, on average, perhaps one demo tape a week, often none at all. The ones that did arrive, he recalled, would come with lengthy, amusing letters with photos and potted biogs, tracing the fledgling band's influences, setting out their aims. The letters, he observed dryly, were often better than the actual tapes. Post-punk, however, he was getting more than a dozen demo tapes a day. And instead of polite, witty letters, what he got was 'a really scruffy tape wrapped up in bog paper with [the words written on it]: "Here's our tape, if you don't fucking like it, stuff it!"'

The effort of listening was always well rewarded, though, he maintained. He claimed to find nearly half the tapes he heard worth the effort, with one in ten being 'excellent'. He tried to avoid recommending any of the groups he played on the show to record companies or anybody else directly involved in the music business, however; he simply played them on his show and anything that happened after that was out of his hands, he insisted.

That said, the Peel show did not suddenly transmogrify into a punk-only cultural ghetto, as was sometimes later suggested. Far from exclusively featuring new-wave artists, a typical Peel show in the late seventies still strove to reflect a wide sense of diversity, mixing the new sounds of Penetration and the Fall with J.J. Cale, perhaps, or Peter Hammill, plus a session maybe from Wire or Roy Harper, all thrown together in a heady brew that also contained more than a smattering of reggae, the odd sea shanty, plus, for one glorious period in 1978, Vivian Stanshall, formerly of the Bonzo Dog Doo Dah Band, reading from the scandalously surreal journals of Sir Henry Rawlinson of Rawlinson End ('If I had all the money I'd spent on drink ... I'd spend it on drink' etc), also doing the voices of his unhinged wife Great Aunt Florrie, Old Scrotum the ancient retainer, Mrs E, the poisonous cook, and several other unforgettable characters.

Ivor Cutler was another regular guest on the programme throughout this period. Cutler, who had done his first session for Peel in 1969, was born in Glasgow in 1923, and was a sort of proto-punk storyteller, poet, surrealist, songsmith and comic raconteur, who acted as one of the few remaining links between the long-haired, flared-trousered Peel of *The Perfumed Garden* and the new, short-haired, straight-legged-jeans Peel of the punk era. (Though he still remained defiantly bearded, a most un-punk-like facial accoutrement.)

Guitarist Colin Newman, whose band Wire did their first Peel session during this period, later recalled how the band had tried to blindside Peel. 'Instead of the usual four songs of three minutes, we did a twelve-minute song,' he said, 'which was the antithesis of everything the Peel show was about: short, punky, unpretentious. A rumour reached us that he wasn't pleased, but fair play to him, he played it — twice. I would like to think he thought, "What a bunch of chancers," and had a good laugh. He was always incredibly personable, just like some bloke you'd meet down the road.'

John's fondness for reggae – and, in particular, a new British group that he would again become the first Radio 1 DJ to play, Misty In Roots – also began to bear fruit in the late seventies. Everyone from the Clash ('White Man in Hammersmith Palais', 'Police and Thieves') to Elvis Costello ('Watching the Detectives'), the Stranglers ('Peaches') and even a group of middle-class musos looking for the main chance called the Police was showing reggae influences that it's hard to believe would have been nearly so manifest had it not been for the Peel show's groundbreaking championing of the music as far back as 1974. Even Bob Marley felt sufficiently convinced by the parallel Peel was clearly drawing between the ghetto roots of reggae and the urban poverty of punk to record his own special tribute, the 'Punky Reggae Party' single, in 1978, which of course Peel played immediately.

One of John's 'top ten favourite sessions of all time' were the two now legendary recordings the Slits made for him in 1977 and 1978. An all-female group of frankly amateur musicians whose teenage singer, Ari

Up, described herself as a 'white Rastafarian', the Slits somehow managed to make the idea of a collision between punk and reggae work in all sorts of rhythmically (and lyrically) unfeasible ways. 'It was their inability to play versus their great determination to play' that made them so fascinating, said John. Destined to be repeated on the show many times over the years, he would always recall the two sessions as 'just magical, I thought.'

As always, not every show ran smoothly. There were John's own occasional mistakes, and then there were frustrating episodes like the time the Clash let them down. Booked for a session on the show in 1979, 'They did half of one,' John said, 'and then amazingly said that the equipment in the studio wasn't up to the standards that they'd expected so they couldn't complete the session. Which seemed to me to be unbearably pretentious of them ...'

Clash tour manager Johnny Green, who was with the band in the studio, remembers things somewhat differently, however. 'The Clash were actually very gung-ho about the prospect of doing their first Peel session,' he maintains. 'But they totally misread the situation and started laying down backing tracks and farting around as though they were making an album. Mick Jones immediately assumed the role of producer and started telling the BBC engineers what to do, which created a very bad atmosphere. Mick didn't mean to rub anybody up the wrong way, though, he just approached the whole thing the wrong way.

'I forget how many tracks they were supposed to record, three or four, but they were taking so long that the BBC engineers started warning them they were going to run out of time. But Jonesy just talked them down. He didn't realise that it wasn't like when they made an album. They should have just gone in and bashed out the tunes as though they were doing them live – bang, bang, bang, in and out again. But they were also smoking a lot of dope, and while that tended to act as fuel for Strummer and Jones, it did mean they neglected the details, shall we say, sometimes. In the end, the inevitable happened and we ran out of time. The engineers got up and left for their tea break or whatever and we packed up and went home.

'Afterwards the band was very upset about it, actually – particularly Mick, who really did think he'd blown it. Word came back that Peel was well pissed off with them, and that upset them even more, because Mick and Joe really understood the value and prestige attached to the Peel show. When the programme they should have been on eventually went out, I remember he laid into them on air. Not viciously, but in his usual sardonic way. I can't remember his exact words but it was something along the lines of, "We should have had the Clash on tonight too but unfortunately they elected not to be here." Some little dig like that.'

Green recalls, however, that John was not one for bearing a grudge for long. 'When he was later given some rough cuts of the band's film *Rude Boy* with some music and snatches of dialogue between, he talked about it on the show and even said he quite liked it. Which just shows you the measure of the man. He might have been left feeling disappointed by some of the musicians he worked with over the years, but he rarely held it against them for long, not as long as he still liked the music.'

John also, memorably, discovered and gave first plays in the late seventies to both Manchester's the Fall and Derry's the Undertones – both bands he would make famous, in different ways, and two of the names that would become practically synonymous with the Peel name for ever after. The Fall – a band I had also worked with, briefly, at Step Forward Records, in 1978, and therefore shared the excitement of hearing Peel play for the first time – was fronted by Mark E. Smith, possibly the most cantankerous, certainly one of the most prolifically talented, singer-songwriters of his generation. Repelling as many, possibly more, people than they would ever entice into buying one of their albums, the Fall would eventually record twenty-three Peel sessions, their last in March 2003 – more sessions than any other group in the history of the programme.

The Undertones were another huge Peel favourite but an entirely different kettle of punk-fish. Once again, in a strange echo of the time he first heard that 'Ride A White Swan' had gone to No. 2, John was driving in the car the first time he ever heard the lead track from the band's first, independently produced (natch) EP, 'Teenage Kicks' on daytime radio. 'It was on the Peter Powell show,' he recalled. John had given Powell, then one of the stars of Radio 1's daytime schedules, his own copy of the record with a note on which he had scribbled the words: 'Peter, this is the one.' Once again, John was so overcome with emotion when he heard Powell play it on his show, he had to pull the car over while he wiped the tears from his eyes. In later years, he claimed that the same emotions would overwhelm him every time he heard the record. He even went so far as to claim that he would like the opening line of the song – 'Teenage dreams/ So hard to beat' – as the epitaph on his gravestone.

Ultimately, whatever he played – or just as pointedly from here on in, didn't play – it was John's own straight-talking but always welcoming personality that held the whole thing together, that helped make sense of it all. Since they had begun working together in the early seventies, Peel and Walters had always put the show together the same way, and despite John's almost obsessive new interest in punk, they continued to do so now. The DJ would submit a list to his producer every afternoon with sometimes as many as 150 suggestions for what to play on the show that night. Walters would then sit down and build the programme around a running order of his own choosing. The first time John knew exactly what he was going to be playing on the show that night, and in what order, would be after he was woken from his now customary pre-show nap.

In many cases, John's list would already be so heavily annotated – three asterisks for a 'must play' – that the most urgent selections became self-evident. All Walters had to do apart from trim the list was perhaps find two tracks with something in common – sometimes just a word in the title – to give John something to work with when he came to do his live links. Not that John was ever short of anything to say about the music he played. However, when, in 1983, Trevor Dann temporarily took over as producer, he suggested John might like to choose the tracks and assemble the running order himself. Dann recently recalled how 'John looked at me with the grateful eyes of a kid meeting Santa and thanked me as effusively as if I'd given him a new toy.'

As the audience for the show continued to get younger – after punk 'the audience demographics completely switched overnight,' John recalled – so older critics took to ridiculing the new format, pointing out that Peel was old enough to have fathered most of the new young artists he was now so avidly interested in. The most striking example of this was the publication in November 1978 of *The Boy Looked At Johnny: An Obituary of Rock'n'roll*, the scurrilous book by Tony Parsons and his then wife, Julie Burchill, in which they gleefully tore to shreds practically every punk icon of the era. John was particularly aggrieved to find himself savaged not because of the music he played but on the basis, it seemed, of simply being too old. As John, who had recently turned forty, later complained to the authors' fellow *NME* scribe, Paul Morley: 'People are appalled when other people are discriminated against on grounds of sex or race or religion, but it seems perfectly all right to discriminate against them on grounds of age. I feel that if I do get the elbow from Radio 1, which I must ultimately do, it will be on the grounds of my age rather than I'm not doing my job well.'

Not long afterwards, John's tenure at *Sounds* came to an abrupt and unpleasant end after the mag's then self-styled punk troubleshooter, Dave McCullough, took Peel to task in one of his weekly us-against-them diatribes, making comments about the show that John found impossible to ignore. He resigned from his column in *Sounds* forthwith and never wrote anything for the mag again.

Geoff Barton, who was deputy editor of *Sounds* at the time, remembers the incident well. 'Essentially, I think McCullough accused him of being a boring old fart, but put in somewhat stronger terms. McCullough was chief of the punk police by then on *Sounds* and I think the fact that John was on Radio 1 made him the enemy in

Dave's eyes, despite all the exposure it had given punk. It was as ridiculous as that, but it upset Peely a great deal and so he decided to resign. It was quite a blow for the mag. I remember Alan on the phone to John pleading for him to reconsider. Alan even got him up to the office and they went to the pub together. I happened to be there, too, and it was quite a sad little scene, Alan and Peely in the corner locked in talks. But John stood firm, it was obviously a matter of strong principle for him.'

Alan Lewis: 'It's true what Geoff says about the McCullough incident – it certainly upset John greatly. That said, my own memory was that John was already finding it hard to do the column anyway. He was so busy and we were always biting our nails over when the copy would arrive. Sometimes we'd already be at the printers, and he would cycle in with it at the last possible moment. McCullough writing spiteful nonsense wouldn't have been enough on its own to make him leave, I'm sure, because he had stood up to so much criticism throughout his career. But he had turned forty and, frankly, I think he was tired of doing it. I don't think he really enjoyed the college gigs any more either but the money was so good he couldn't turn them down. So he already had a lot on and writing for *Sounds* was always more a labour of love. I think we only paid him about fifty pounds a week for the column. The McCullough thing was simply the last straw.'

Meanwhile, John Walters, he once confessed to me over a pint, still spent 'far too much of my time convincing the powers that be just to leave Peely alone and let him get on with it. They just don't get it and they never will. I tell them the Peel show is the best thing on the bloody radio and they look at me like I must be an even bigger lunatic than him. But then it sort of goes hand in hand with the job – the moment they do understand would probably be the moment to end the show.'

As Alan Lewis says now: 'John would be the first to acknowledge that, like all great men, he owed his success to a certain degree of luck, and to some extent the structure of the BBC itself. Being a publicly funded broadcaster, they had had the luxury of setting up the station the way they wanted it, but they knew they had to find a slot for someone like Peel, even if they would not have had him within a million miles of one of their big daytime shows. The BBC needed to be seen to be covering as many kinds of popular music as possible, even when they couldn't stand the stuff, and John fitted that remit perfectly. By the end of the seventies, even the BBC had woken up to the fact that he also brought with him a certain amount of prestige, though they would have been loath to admit it, especially after he started devoting so much of his show to that ghastly new punk stuff.'

But if John sometimes felt alienated and

misunderstood, he knew he could always rely on the redoubtable Walters for reassurance and support, even if that meant no more than a few bottles of red at the nearby Indian restaurant that had become their second home. Walters, for all his bluff and bluster, had proved to be a staunch ally and loyal friend. As one of the most vocal defenders of public service broadcasting, he continued to watch Peel's back, defending him to whoever listened, as well as those that did not, that John's was 'the most original voice in broadcasting.'

As Peel later said, 'I just concentrate on playing the records, and leave all the business stuff to Walters.' He jokingly characterised their relationship as being that of 'the organ-grinder and the monkey. With each one believing the other to be the monkey.' Another time he described the relationship as 'like a man and his dog – only each of us thinks the other is the dog.' Whichever it was, it certainly appeared to be working well.

CHAPTER THREE

God, an Informal Pose

In the early 1980s, John Peel stuck up a photo of Liverpool legend Kenny Dalglish on his studio wall, with a handwritten caption: 'God, an informal pose.' It was not meant ironically. By then, however, Peel could empathise – accustomed, as he now was, to being feted as a god in his own right – on the radio.

The Peel show came to exemplify everything that was interesting and innovative about music in the eighties, just as his previous shows had accurately reflected the true mood of their times. The names recurring with most frequency on his programmes were now Joy Division, the Cure, Orange Juice, the Teardrop Explodes and, later, the Smiths and the birth of the whole Madchester scene epitomised by 'baggy' progenitors the Happy Mondays.

As Bernard Sumner, formerly of Joy Division, now New Order, said recently: 'If it wasn't for John Peel, there would [have been] no Joy Division and no New Order.' Bassist Peter Hook added: 'His was the only show that you could be satisfied by and infuriated by within the same hour. He was immune to fashion; he just liked what he liked. That's why people loved him – he took chances, and people these days very rarely take chances. Peel was the first person to put us on the radio – we sent him a demo and he became a patron to New Order and Joy Division. It was a long time before we actually met him. We were nervous – we had to have a couple of drinks. [But] he was nervous about meeting us, which flabbergasted us.'

Andy McCluskey of eighties synth-pop hit-makers Orchestral Manoeuvres in the Dark echoed those sentiments, acknowledging that 'John Peel played a single but crucial role in my early career. He played our first single, "Electricity", on his evening show and thanks to him it sold out its first 5,000 run within a week.' While Smiths guitarist Johnny Marr later claimed: 'The Smiths' early success was largely due to the John Peel show. We would try out new songs on the sessions and these often were the definitive version. John Peel was always the best around.'

John also continued to support the underdogs at the indie labels, too. Geoff Travis of Rough Trade says now: 'Without John, I don't think Rough Trade would have been able to grow and support the artists we have. Most of our bands did their first radio session with him: the Fall, the Blue Orchids, the Smiths ...' Peel also famously gave a first session to Sheffield's Pulp as far back as 1981. 'Giving Jarvis Cocker a session when he was still a schoolboy changed the course of his life,' added

Travis. Cocker had shoved a cassette into Peel's hands as he left the stage after another roadshow at Sheffield University. 'He said, "Thanks, I'll listen to that in the car." Then a few days later his producer rang up asking if we'd like to do a session on the show ...'

Peel's pick of the original Pulp session was 'Turkey Mambo', which he later rated alongside 'Shoplifting' from the May '78 Slits session as one of his top ten all-time favourite session moments. Stunned and grateful though he was at the time, Cocker later ruefully admitted that, in retrospect, he almost wished the band hadn't been given a Peel session so early. Instead of being besieged by offers from impressed record company bigwigs, or even indie little wigs, 'nothing happened – for years.' In fact, it was twelve years before their next Peel session, in 1993, and another two years before they finally broke through to a wider audience with the sublime hit single 'Common People'.

John's reputation as the most important DJ breaking unsigned acts was now such that in 1983 the then unsigned Billy Bragg drove to the Radio 1 studios with a mushroom biryani and a copy of his record after hearing Peel mention that he was hungry. The subsequent airplay from the thoroughly impressed DJ launched Bragg's career. While Kevin Shields of My Bloody Valentine recalls how 'in 1985 we went and stood outside the BBC with the first record we made, 'cos he often said he played records given to him outside. I think we were there for four hours because we hadn't worked out what time he arrived. [When he eventually came out] he said, "Is this any good?" and we said, "Yes." We listened every night until he played it, but we would have anyway. John Peel was our universe for a long time.'

The excellence of so many sessions led to a series of albums in the eighties, 'The Peel Sessions' (on the Strange Fruit label). Guitarist Will Sergeant of Liverpudlian Peel favourites Echo and the Bunnymen said: 'He was enormously influential in bringing the Bunnymen to the public. You can't imagine us getting anywhere without having done the early Peel sessions. We treated them as demos too, they were dead important for us in discovering and recording our sound. But he was more than that. He was important as a fan, because everyone listened to him. The first time I heard the Residents was on John Peel, and I thought, "What the hell's this?" His programme was like a religion; you'd listen to it to hear what was about and what was coming up.'

The Bunnymen would record several sessions for the Peel show in the eighties, including, most poignantly perhaps, when they performed at his sixtieth birthday party and the tears, as ever, came to his eyes. 'He still played our new records,' says Sergeant, 'but he was always one for keeping the programme fresh. He was a bit like a schoolteacher in that he'd help you and send you on your way into the world and then a new batch of pupils would arrive. I remember when we did our first Peel session he said, "And here we have the mighty Echo and the Bunnymen," and we were so chuffed. We all crowded round our trannies. It felt like we meant something …'

He was never afraid to send himself up, however. More embarrassing even than miming the mandolin with Rod Stewart on *Top of the Pops* all those years ago was his appearance in the mid-eighties on an edition of *The Old Grey Whistle Test*, where, for reasons probably best forgotten, Walters had corralled John and various other Radio 1 DJs into taking part in an impromptu skiffle band. Thumping away on tea-chest bass, John wore his usual hangdog look, squirming with embarrassment. As a Radio 1 DJ, he was reconciled, he said, to being involved occasionally in 'ludicrous things'. There were also Radio 1 Fun Weeks, 'which usually consisted of travelling the country with a bunch of other DJs, and Noel Edmonds filling people's hotel rooms with chickens. In more enlightened days than ours you'd be burnt at the stake for doing that. People like Mike Read and DLT would often complain that they couldn't go anywhere without being recognised, but of course would go everywhere in a tartan suit carrying a guitar, so they would have attracted attention in a lunatic asylum.'

Most important, he still retained his radical edge. The

new Radio 1 breakfast presenter, Mike Read, might have complained on his show about Frankie Goes to Hollywood's 'Relax' being on the Radio 1 playlist in 1983, but Peel had had the band for a live session of the song long before the record was even recorded. His show provided a refreshing, much-needed counterpoint to the increasingly bland fare of the charts in the eighties, as synth-drums and faceless wizard-producers began to dominate the pop charts, and the emphasis, as with everything else in the climactic Thatcher years, was placed more than ever on the big and the showy. In contrast, Peel became a great supporter of obscure movements, almost single-handedly creating the 'Norwich scene' of 1983–84, which featured such mini-treasures as the Higsons, the Farmer's Boys and Serious Drinking.

As Walters increasingly moved on to other pet projects in the eighties, a succession of younger, well-meaning but clearly misguided producers would suggest to John that the new generation of Smiths and New Order fans might occasionally want to hear something by older, similarly minded if now distant musical cousins – like Van Morrison in his younger, more agitated days, perhaps, or even Bowie (whose experimental albums with Eno in Berlin in the late seventies had clearly had an influence on New Order and others). But John always refused point-blank. Those artists already received more than their share of airplay, he argued. He was only interested in the stuff the rest of the gang weren't playing – or at least, not yet. In an era of Gary Davies in the morning, Jakki Brambles at lunchtime, and Steve Wright in the afternoon, Peel was still more interested in playing music than selling joke books.

As a result, John became almost as famous in the eighties for the bands he turned down for sessions as those he gave airtime to, saying *non, merci* at different times to such future mega-stars as the Police, U2, and Charlie Gillett discovery Dire Straits. Peel left bands like that, he said, to other Radio 1 DJs such as Andy Peebles, whose new early-evening show now acted as a useful link between the Kid Jensen drive-time show and Peel's very different late-night programme. In fact, Peel favoured the new evening line-up over any other he had been part of at Radio 1 until then. The Peebles show kept the jokey banter to a minimum and concentrated on playing a good mix of new chart and non-chart music, ending with something suitably 'outré' each night before handing over to Peel at ten. It meant that for the first time in its history Radio 1's daytime schedule actually dovetailed nicely into the Peel show, and for seven and a half hours – from four thirty till midnight – Radio 1 would actually be in a position to offer systematic, cohesive music programming. The rest of the daytime output was still weighed down more than ever by nostalgia, competitions and vacuous chatter, but for now Peel owned the night.

A new generation of Radio 1 DJs was arriving – mainstream presenters like Andy Peebles, Mike Read, David 'Kid' Jensen and Peter Powell, who actually cared about the music their programmes featured along with all the usual daytime razzmatazz. Though bound by their strict playlists, DJs like Jensen and Powell still insisted on squeezing in occasional non-playlist songs, many recommended to them by Peel (as happened, most memorably, of course, in the case of Powell with 'Teenage Kicks').

John's ever more extreme musical tastes – as well as the occasional sardonic put-down on air – still sometimes brought him into conflict with other more conservative DJs at the BBC, such as 'the hairy cornflake', Dave Lee Travis, and Simon Bates, who had replaced the now-departed Tony Blackburn as Peel's number-one hate figure at the station. Peel and Jensen were such good pals that they once hid in a car park together, after a drunken office Christmas party, waiting for Bates to come outside so they could beat him up. Fortunately, or not as the case may be, Bates never showed. Later, in the early nineties, as a special Christmas treat one year, John famously went to see Bates in panto with Andy Kershaw, 'just so we could boo and hiss,' Kershaw later told me with a snigger.

Unlike ten years before, however, there was now less

hostility to his programme behind the scenes. Things were definitely 'moving in the right direction,' he claimed in the *NME*. He added that he now felt confident that if he were to drop dead, 'a certain amount of the slack would be taken up by some of the other [DJs]. Two or three years ago that wouldn't have been true.'

A typical show in the early eighties might comprise Swell Maps, the Quads, the Jam, Phillip Goodhand-Tait, XTC, Misty In Roots and a session from the Cure, perhaps, all shuffled with the informal ease Peel was now famous for. He talked a lot less than he used to in his links but the clipped brevity gave a sharper sense of his understated but wickedly cutting humour. Benjamin Zephaniah recalled hearing one of Misty In Roots' records for the first time on the Peel show. 'He didn't do any big build-up, like "And now some reggae!" He just introduced it like any other record on his show: "And this is Misty In Roots ..." I thought, wow, white people like our music!'

That said, John would also cheerfully admit sometimes that if it was up to him, the new Undertones or Fall album would probably get played in its entirety every night. 'What I feel about [those bands] ... it's love really,' he stuttered. 'It is. It's the same as I feel about Liverpool. It transcends reason and it's just a passion.'

The mid-eighties also saw the Peel show embrace New York hip-hop for the first time, which led to equal exposure for early Chicago house, Detroit techno and a new-found passion for what he endearingly termed in the early days the 'African pop' of artists like Fela Kuti and the Bhundu Boys. Once again, senior BBC management were perplexed. 'Someone from management did come down when I was playing a lot of hip-hop, and then later when I was playing jungle, to inform me that I shouldn't be playing this music,' John later recalled, adding with astonishment and no little rancour, 'because it was the music of the black criminal classes.'

Geoff Barton recalls meeting Peel again during this period – and finding him 'completely unchanged, still as ready to stick by his guns as ever.' It was 1983 and Barton, who had recently succeeded Alan Lewis as *Sounds* editor, had been invited to be a guest on Radio 1's then regular Friday evening show, *Roundtable*, in which guests would review some of the week's new releases. The show was presented by Richard Skinner and joining him and Geoff that week were Peel and the singer Sheena Easton.

Barton: 'I remember taking an instant dislike to Easton; she seemed like a hard-faced Scotswoman and we didn't get on at all. But Peely was charm personified, which was a real measure of the man. It didn't matter that he didn't personally like her music, he was amusing, polite, attentive, and she absolutely loved him! He had her eating out of his hands.

'I also saw another side of John on that occasion, too. There was a single by ex-Deep Purple singer Ian Gillan amongst the pile and when we came to it I mentioned that coincidentally we had a Gillan feature in the new issue of *Sounds* that week and people should go and buy it, sort of tongue-in-cheek but giving it a good-natured plug too. Then during the break while the record was playing Skinner went absolutely mad at me! "Who do you think you are? You can't plug your magazine, you wanker!" Really stroppy. I'd never done one of these programmes before and didn't know the rules so I was apologetic, I really hadn't meant any harm.

'But Peel stood up for me and really took Skinner to task. "Leave him alone," John told him. "He's only doing his job; why shouldn't he mention his magazine? Now shut up!" And Skinner did, he never said another word about it and we went on with the show as though nothing had happened. I already had a lot of admiration for John Peel, but I had even more after that. He really was a very sincere and special person.'

John certainly had his spiky side. He introduced Queen on *Top of the Pops* in 1984 as 'the boys from Sun City', after the band had defied the international apartheid ban and played at the infamous 'leisure resort' in South Africa.

In 1983, Radio 1 staged a week's programming from Liverpool. As part of the broadcast, it was suggested that John might like to make an introductory programme about his home city. Persuading him to stroll about the city with a portable recording team was not easy. This was many years before he became expert at non-music programming, but he was finally persuaded to give it a bash on condition that his daughter and her teenage Goth friend could accompany him. The result was a fascinating programme in which Peel took the listener back to the Liverpool he knew, pointing out various landmarks along the way, including the Royal London Insurance office where his brother Alan then worked.

Peel always maintained a distance from the artists he featured. He was almost boastful of the fact that none of his really close friends now had anything to do with the music business. 'I think knowing amazingly few people in bands helps me keep my perspective,' he said, not unreasonably. However, Captain Beefheart did still phone him once a year, usually a few weeks before his birthday. 'I'm always really frightened when he does because I never know what to say to him,' he chuckled. 'You always think that what you're saying is so banal and stupid that he must be thinking, "Why do I bother phoning this fella?"' He only met Mark E. Smith of the Fall a couple of times, too, so could hardly describe him as a friend, either. 'When I do see him I never know what to say to him anyway, so we just punch each other on the shoulder in a manly way and go our separate ways.'

He would recount the story of the time Mike Read had insisted on dragging him to a then fashionable nightclub in Bond Street. 'He was immediately surrounded by all sorts of glamorous women. It was one of those places where they have an area where only top celebs can go, and Bryan Ferry came down ... I could see him looking across this glamorous crowd at me – looking like the man who'd come to collect the empties.'

Although he cut down his live appearances in the late eighties, for many years John compered both the Reading and Glastonbury Festivals. He also loved going to Holland, where for a time he regularly hosted the annual Pink Pop Festival. He claimed that the Dutch liked him because John Peel translated as John Prick. But his fear of flying, which seemed to get worse the older he got, meant he was becoming more choosy about where he went and what he agreed to do.

Most devastating of all, he developed a deep and abiding fear of large crowds after being at the Heysel Stadium in Belgium in 1985, when fighting amongst Liverpool and Juventus supporters before the start of the European Cup final led to the collapse of a wall and the deaths of thirty-nine fans, mostly Italian. Then, just four years later, in April 1989, Liverpool met Nottingham Forest in the semi-final of the FA Cup at Hillsborough, Sheffield, and ninety-six Liverpool fans – men, women and children – were crushed to death before the start of the match when overcrowding on the terraces led to pandemonium. John opened his first show after the news was broadcast with Aretha Franklin's version of the Anfield anthem 'You'll Never Walk Alone'.

Spider Stacy, of the Pogues, recalled bumping into John at a gig at Dingwalls in London not long after the Heysel tragedy. 'Of course, being a Liverpool fan he was gutted and probably not too focused on what we were saying. But I just wanted to say thanks because he did so much for so many bands.' John didn't really hear him, though. He was still thinking of Heysel.

John also became one of the *Observer*'s chief music critics in the eighties. It was the first time since he regularly reviewed the singles for *Sounds* in the early seventies that John had put his thoughts down on paper about music and it produced some hilarious results. At a Dire Straits show in June 1988, he quipped: 'Sometimes the music became so lush that I felt as though I was being force-fed Swiss roll.' At a Wet Wet Wet show the same month he described being amongst the crowd as like being 'in the company of some of the extrovert members of the 18–30 holiday scene, noisy lads reeking of lager, giggling lasses awash with parfum.'

Restricted to only the artists the paper deemed appropriate for their readership, the reviews also gave a fascinating insight into John's broader view of pop music – and pop life – in general. For example, reviewing Wham!'s final concert at Wembley Stadium, in July 1986, he wrote: 'They never wearied of the flirtations and the running about, and when Elton John appeared in an asinine clown's outfit – does he do these things to mask some insecurity? – they correctly perceived that this was an honour for him rather than Wham!' While in May 1987, the music at a Pretenders concert was so 'dogmatic and humourless' it left the audience 'amusing themselves by punching balloons about in a thoughtful manner, while otherwise behaving as though attending a lecture on the inland waterways of Belgium.'

Madonna at Wembley stadium in August that year also received the gimlet eye of Peel's wit. 'At 8.18, Madonna appeared, wearing the fortified liberty bodice that has thrilled millions worldwide. "Thank you and hello, London," she improvised ...' Bob Dylan also came in for some jovially applied stick. 'Being an enigma at twenty is fun, being an enigma at thirty shows a lack of imagination, and being an enigma at Dylan's age is just plain daft. From the moment the living legend took to the stage, it was evident that here was business he wanted accomplished with the minimum of effort.'

When occasionally presented with an artist he actually admired, he could, of course, be equally erudite. Reviewing Echo & the Bunnymen in January 1988, he concluded: 'You will not, unless you search a well-stocked broom cupboard, spot many Will Sergeant look-alikes, but guitarist Will was, reluctant though I am to single out individuals after a first-class team performance, my Man of the Match.' Shirley Bassey came in for unexpected praise in May 1988. 'With arms outstretched ... the Welsh thrush radiates a preposterous intimacy, scampering through a routine with which everyone seems totally familiar and at ease. To have attempted anything other than surrender would have been churlish.'

In the summer of 1985, Peel and Walters were asked to squeeze a new face into their cramped, untidy office – that of latest Radio 1 recruit, Andy Kershaw, from Rochdale. The twenty-five-year-old Lancastrian had come to the station via *The Old Grey Whistle Test*, where he had been one of the new young presenters (along with Mark Ellen and David Hepworth) who had replaced Bob Harris, whose TV credibility withered on the vine in the glare of punk, which Bob, in fairness, never pretended to like let alone understand. Kershaw was different. Raised on the raw, high-minded principles of the new wave, he and Peel hit it off immediately, the older DJ becoming a friend and mentor to the man who would increasingly come to be seen as the sorcerer's apprentice. In fact, Kershaw often poked fun at John, saying he was like Eeyore from *Winnie the Pooh*. In which case, John would reply, Kershaw must be Tigger.

Kershaw admits now that he was 'hugely fortunate' to be taken under the expansive Peel wing. 'What better education?' he said. Peel had been Kershaw's chief musical influence since his teens. 'Then suddenly, blow me, I was sharing his ten-foot by ten-foot office space, having to sit on an upturned litter bin.' If John felt somewhat unsettled by the arrival of a colleague young enough to be his son, he did his best not to show it. 'Once he realised I was a huge admirer and that we shared many of the same tastes, we became big pals.'

Kershaw would write later of how the two would stroll down to Stern's African record shop together, just behind Broadcasting House, and buy piles of records on spec, then spend 'a wonderful afternoon finding out what we'd bought, like a couple of kids in the playground swapping bubble-gum cards.' They even began holidaying together, attending the annual TT races in the Isle of Man. Peel was simply 'the most natural broadcaster' Kershaw had ever known. 'He taught me to talk to listeners as though you're talking to one person.' The highest accolade he could pay, he added, was that away from the microphone John was 'exactly the same as he was when he was in front of it.'

For a while, Andy's show used to follow on from John's, their shows dovetailing superbly across the entire spectrum of esoteric music around the world – and some other places too, by the sounds of it some nights. The cross-pollination of music and ideas was unlike any other previously enjoyed by two Radio 1 shows (aside from the aural wallpaper of daytime). As time passed, Kershaw's show tended to feature more roots and world music, while Peel still made room for whatever flight of eccentricity he had unearthed that week. It made for the best four hours to be found anywhere on radio in the late eighties and early nineties. Even their handovers were unique. Eschewing the usual 'madcap' chat DJs were expected to indulge in at such moments, they kept things to a parched, often hilarious minimum, concluding surreally towards the end of their run together by simply burbling the words 'Matey DJ banter, matey DJ banter' at each other.

'Peel introduced me to so many kinds of music ... He was a broadcaster, not a narrowcaster.' To have been put in the care of Peel and Walters, two of the all-time great champions of public service broadcasting, he added, 'was a fantastic induction and education. It was hilarious, too; they were like panto dames.'

In August 1989, John reached fifty years of age. To mark this landmark – he was now officially the oldest DJ on Radio 1 – he was invited to be that week's guest on Radio 4's *Desert Island Discs*. Despite stating on the programme that playing records for a living was his 'way of going out into the streets and righting those wrongs I think should be righted,' he surprised many longstanding fans with some of his choices.

'It's Over' by Roy Orbison was not unexpected, as

he'd played it on his own shows often enough over the years. (He described hearing it again recently while standing alone at fogbound Stowmarket station waiting for the train to London. The sound was coming from a nearby industrial estate and for a moment it had brought tears to his sentimental old eyes, he said.) The inclusion of Jimmy Reed's 'Too Much', the Undertones' 'Teenage Kicks' and the Fall's 'Eat Y'self Fitter' were equally unsurprising. Eyebrows remained firmly raised, however, when he asked for Rachmaninov's second piano concerto, Handel's 'Zadok the Priest' (recorded at the coronation of George VI) and 'Pasi Pano Pane Zviedzo' by the Four Brothers.

John later confessed in the *Guardian* that the problem was an 'overpowering urge to pick a track or two to convince sceptical Radio 4 listeners that you are not the cultural wasteland they probably perceive you to be. Thus, I played Handel's "Zadok the Priest" on *Desert Island Discs*, but have yet to introduce it to clubland. The same is true of Roy Orbison's "It's Over". Unequalled as Roy is for singing along with in the car (minor blood vessels snapping in the forehead as you strive for, but fall short of, those high notes) he doesn't, evidence has shown, do it for crowds of sweaty young people, wild-eyed on drink and other exhilarants. Not yet anyway.'

Interviewed ten years later, he claimed his real all-time favourite records included some of the following:

an obscure Jagger–Richards song, 'I'd Rather Be Out With the Boys', originally recorded by mid-sixties Manchester 'no-hit wonders, the Toggery Five'; a reggae version of Paul Simon's 'Richard Cory' by Jamaican singer Yami Bolo, who, not understanding the words, called it 'Richer Cory'; Stanley Winston's early seventies soul ballad 'No More Ghettos in America' ('This guy made this one forty-five and the first thirty seconds eclipses Mick Hucknall's entire output,' said John); and 'You'd Better Move On', the r&b classic by Arthur Alexander, given to him by a girlfriend all those years ago in Texas. It was, he mused, 'Her way of saying, "Suit action to the title, fat boy".'

After John's *Desert Island Discs* appearance was broadcast, the novelist Anthony Powell wrote to John thanking him for choosing his novel sequence *A Dance to the Music of Time* as his desert-island reading. (His other literary interests were the works of Captain W. E. Johns, creator of Biggles and the pioneering aviatrix Worrals.)

After the recording was completed, John found himself obliged to accompany the programme's presenter, the charming Sue Lawley, to a BBC dinner at which they were seated at a table alongside other prominent guests, including the BBC's Royal and Diplomatic correspondent, Nicholas Witchell, mystery novelist P. D. James and the pianist Jonathan Powell. John instinctively turned to the man sitting next to him and introduced himself. 'Hello, I'm John Peel,' he said chummily. To which he received the frosty riposte: 'I'm John Birt [then Director General of the BBC] and actually we were introduced five minutes ago outside.' John later said that he never really recovered from that – another lesson harshly learned, thus reinforcing his long-held view that attending such 'celebrity' functions was simply not for him.

By the early nineties, although he was only a year older than John, Walters was ready to retire, having given Radio 1 the last twenty-five years of his life. He also wanted to stretch his wings as a broadcaster, having presented for some time his own weekly arts programme on Radio 1, *Walters' Weekly*. Peel himself was not quite ready to quit yet, though. His new *Who's Who* entry may have listed his recreations as 'making plans to go and live in France [and] staring out of the window,' but instead he simply carried on producing the show himself, backed up by a small two-person team, now young enough to be his grandchildren. But then, so too were most of the artists he was featuring on his show.

John was also still broadcasting his Festive Fifty in the early nineties, something that he'd been doing since 1976 and which had become an annual tradition. A countdown of the best tracks of the year as voted for by the listeners to his show, the Festive Fifty became seen as a prestige end-of-year berth, particularly for bands on independent labels. He once famously bumped the

Dawn Parade from the top spot because of obvious vote-rigging via the internet. He did place them at No. 50, though, 'for their sheer cheek.' Despite Peel's eclectic playlist, the yearly countdown did tend to be composed largely of indie artists, something he complained about on air but to no avail. In 1991, the year Nirvana's 'Smells Like Teen Spirit' single topped the Festive Fifty, he grew so exasperated of 'white boys with guitars' that he actually cancelled the whole thing in a huff. He later relented, however, and agreed to play the countdown one record at a time, one week at a time, throughout the first fifty weeks of 1992. He dubbed it 'the Phantom Fifty'. In 1997, he would broadcast a Festive 31, in protest at the comparative paucity of votes that year.

When John was awarded the prestigious Sony Award for Broadcaster of the Year in 1993, he went to the podium intending to give a speech paying tribute to Sheila. But as he stepped up and began thinking about delivering the speech, he burst into tears. Speech abandoned. 'To see it written down would probably make people's toes curl, but Sheila really is the fuel on which I run,' he explained apologetically afterwards. When, in 1994, the *NME* presented him with the award for Godlike Genius at their annual ceremony, he again wept on stage as he gave his acceptance speech. He also came top in the Best DJ category eleven times in the annual *Melody Maker* readers' poll throughout this period.

Nevertheless, the music press still occasionally gave him a hard time. John was particularly upset when he was the target for *Q* magazine's notoriously snide 'Who The Hell Does [Insert Name] Think They Are?', mainly because he and Sheila had welcomed the writer and photographer to their home so warmly, treating them to lunch and introducing them to the children. 'Then they went away and wrote this rather spiteful piece in which they took the piss out of all of us, including my dad, who's dead, and that didn't do an awful lot to cheer me up.'

When, in 1994, the new director of BBC Radio and controller of Radio 1, Matthew Bannister, embarked on his night of the long knives, in which most of the existing high-profile DJs were sacked, Peel and Kershaw were part of only a small handful of DJs to survive the cull. Gone suddenly were smarmy old vets like Simon Bates, Steve Wright and Dave Lee Travis, and for a time Peel and Kershaw rejoiced in the fact that soon all programmes on Radio 1 would sound like theirs. It was a forlorn hope. Bannister received fierce criticism from within and outside the BBC for his decision, and had to suffer DLT airing his grievances live on air during his final show, and Bates and others crying foul in the press.

With listening figures plummeting dramatically, Radio 1 quickly turned to Chris Evans to relaunch their breakfast show and peppered the rest of the daytime schedule with what amounted, ultimately, to little more than an updated version of what had gone before – chirpy, cheerful, 'young' presenters spinning the hits of the day and running listener-friendly quizzes and competitions. The lone exception was the excellent new afternoon show presented by Mark Radcliffe and Lard (Marc Riley), who had until then been part of the evening schedule.

But if the new regime were quickly hedging their bets, Bannister claimed at the time: 'As long as I have a breath in my body John Peel will be on air.' Though John noted with some scepticism that Bannister had said something very similar about Johnnie Walker, shortly before declining to offer him a new contract. (Walker now presents the drive-time show on Radio 2.) Wholesale change in music was one thing, but abrupt and massive changes in work and in life made him uncomfortable, afraid the baby would be thrown out with the bath water. Fears that were hardly allayed when the axe began to fall on some of the production staff he liked working with. When, in the early nineties, the Peel show was reduced to just two shows a week – a meagre four hours – and shunted to weekends, John thought he could see the writing on the wall. Later in the decade however, he was back to a more welcome and familiar slot (Tuesdays, Wednesdays and Thursdays, from 8.40 p.m. till 10.30 p.m.).

Following on from the new, Britpop-based *Evening*

Session show, presented by former *NME* writer Steve Lamacq and Jo Whiley, a former presenter for *WPFM*, Radio 4's youth culture and music show, the Peel show now found another new young wave of listeners, as many of the Oasis-obsessed listeners from the *Evening Session* stayed on to catch whatever the weird guy started his show with this time – and what he might play next. The same old heavily baited hook Peel had caught all of us on through the years. As Steve Lamacq said: 'You can't listen to someone like John without taking on part of his style. He was groundbreaking for me. He just broke the rules the whole time. He did things that just weren't done. He was a maverick and he got away with it. You have to have trust with a DJ, and everyone built that trust with John.'

Alan McGee, the Glasgow record mogul who discovered Oasis, told *The Times*: 'John Peel played the first band I was in and the first release by Creation Records. Without John, Creation probably wouldn't have happened. Kids listened to him under the bedclothes to hear new music. It was astonishing that he was still so up on new music [in his sixties].'

Grunge progenitors Sonic Youth had done an amazing early session for Peel in 1988, including a version of the Fall's version of the Kinks' 'Victoria', and in November 1989, two years before they released the *Nevermind* album, Peel also gave a first session to Seattle newcomers Nirvana. (Then in the UK for their first, brief, visit, they kicked off with a version of their first single on the independent Sub Pop label, 'Love Buzz'.) But apart from special moments like that – and the occasional crazed release from one of the less feted, more extreme Seattle acts like the Misfits – Peel had very little truck with grunge.

He was famously no slave to Britpop, either, though he did write in the sleeve notes that came with the vinyl version of Elastica's later limited edition *Elasticatalogue* album that the only other band that made him feel the way they did was the Fall. High praise indeed.

'Britpop passed me by entirely,' said John, 'because it didn't sound as good as the stuff they were replicating.' As such, Peel, pointedly, never offered a session to Oasis. 'I never really thought Oasis were much good, to be honest, so they didn't do one. Whereas Blur did a couple of times.' In fact, Blur, who did their first Peel session in the early nineties, gave the lie to the accusation that John always abandoned acts after they became famous, their final session for him taking place in June 1997.

Instead, when he wasn't obsessing over the new Fall album, he found himself suddenly besotted with jungle, drum'n'bass, Pakistani qawwali, Congolese soukous, ambient electronica, death metal and the then new 'alt.country' sound of US acts like Will Oldham, and Whiskeytown and their various offshoots. As Super Furry Animals singer Gruff Rhys recalled:

'[John] was very wary of trends. Even in the middle of a conservative movement like Britpop, he was introducing people to drum'n'bass and techno.'

And, as usual, he also fell head over heels for the usual raggle-taggle collection of indie misfits and post-wave orphans. Gorky's Zygotic Mynci, Welsh-singing five-piece from Pembrokeshire, were one such who tickled John's fancy in the mid-nineties. Led by singer-keyboardist Euros Childs, whose weird, whimsical tunes, such as 'Diamond Dew' and 'Patio Song', were captured in a memorable session, they would prove too wilfully eccentric even for some of Peel's regular listeners. Not so Cornershop, another mid-nineties Peel discovery, who had a No. 1 hit in 1997 with a remixed version (by Fatboy Slim) of one of the tunes first heard on the Peel show, 'Brimful of Asha' (though John professed to be more keen on their Punjabi version of the Beatles' 'Norwegian Wood').

A long-time veteran of the festival, John was equally pleased to be asked to co-present the new BBC TV coverage of Glastonbury, which they began doing each year in the late nineties. A typically understated, Wellington-boots and anorak-clad presence around the site, John exemplified the unpretentious and inclusive spirit of the Glastonbury weekend. As festival organiser Michael Eavis recalled, it was entirely appropriate that Peel should find himself coming full circle almost by introducing Glastonbury to yet another new generation.

'[John] was this young man who first came in 1970, 1971 – he knew what was going on even then,' Eavis said. 'He came from Beatle country, didn't he? Pop music was the first priority for that generation. But he never grew up, he stayed with it, all the way through. In 1983, I was listening to his show and he had the Smiths on. I went to see them in Bristol on the strength of his recommendation, booked them for the festival, and they turned out to be the greatest thing. He had that instinct.'

John was now regularly being sent around two hundred CDs every week, come rain or shine. Plus maybe another hundred singles each week in various seven-inch and twelve-inch formats and attired in all sorts of weird and wonderful sleeves. His philosophy: 'Maybe there's something in here that turns out to be quite wonderful.' As a result, however, he had been forced to have several of the sheds and outhouses where he kept his mountainous collection fitted with reinforcements in order to take the weight of it all.

A large wooden shed opposite the main house was where he kept his vast collection of twelve-inch singles. Another shed, just past the chicken coop, was where he housed all his seven-inch singles. Yet another outside building was where he kept his 'LPs' – estimated to be over thirty thousand strong. Then there were the racks of records that occupied several rooms inside the old garage that now served as his studio whenever he was broadcasting from Peel Acres, as he began to do on a semi-regular basis in the nineties.

Between the racks of records and CDs were decades' worth of football memorabilia, all relating to Liverpool, plus dozens of photographs of Sheila and the children, hundreds of old bike magazines carefully stacked in the corner, some dating back nearly fifty years. The records weren't just tools of the trade, he would point out. They were much more than that. They were, quite literally, he smiled, 'my fortune.'

The farmhouse studio was now where he did most of his production work, too. He still spent 'far too much time in London', but he always made a point of playing all the records at home first. 'As my wife would confirm, I still spend an insane amount of time – six to eight hours a day – listening to records and putting together lists for the show.'

Each record he listened to was dutifully listed on an old-fashioned card index, begun back in the late sixties. He knew he should try transferring it all to a computer, he said, but genuinely felt that with so many years of records to work through, recataloguing it all now 'would almost certainly take the rest of my life.' He had a curator's mindset and never tired of poring over the daily envelopes of new records. 'I'll come in here to find something, and almost always find something else that I've completely forgotten about. It's a great stress-reliever.'

London was now merely the place he went to when he absolutely had to, to broadcast his show. Even a one-night stopover in London was a depressing thought. 'I get incredibly homesick,' he said. 'I can reduce myself to tears just by thinking about my family. It's probably the case that I need treatment of some sort, but I'm not going to take it.'

His unease at being away from home had been considerably heightened since June 1996, when Sheila had suffered a brain haemorrhage and was seriously ill in hospital for weeks. John later claimed that he'd had a premonition something bad was going to happen to her, but dismissed it as just another manifestation of his usual homesickness. When she collapsed and was rushed to hospital, John was actually on the Isle of Man, at the TT races with Andy Kershaw. Andy accompanied him as he raced to be at Sheila's bedside. As they waited nervously for the ferry, John stood on the cliffs 'and just howled into the night.' Thankfully, Andy 'stayed with me all the way to the hospital. I'll never forget how sympathetic, yet firm, he was.' When he got there, John collapsed at Sheila's bedside and wept. Through his tears, he said simply he would have 'no idea what to do' without her. When he finally got her back home to Suffolk he nursed her for weeks himself. 'I have never known fear like it,' he later said. 'I remember the terrible emptiness I felt when the children and I were waiting in the hospital for the brain surgery to finish. I didn't cry – I was somewhere beyond crying.'

Thankfully, the operation proved a success, though there would be a long period of rehabilitation, and Sheila's eyesight would start to slowly deteriorate, too, as a long-term result. It was a dreadful time for Sheila and the family but at least she was alive and well. As a present to cheer her up as she recovered from her illness, John bought her a brand-new hand-made Morgan V8 car from a dealership in north London. 'I bought it and gave it to her in a dramatic and well-staged presentation in a lay-by outside Bury St Edmunds.'

At his sixtieth birthday party in 1999, John boasted that he was 'fully enjoying all the benefits of being a pensioner', not least the £1 off Friday lunch he was now entitled to at the village pub. Fond of reminding people of a family history of early deaths, he commented wryly: 'In actuarial terms, I only have about seven or eight years left.' Adding, optimistically, that he hoped he'd cheated his genetic heritage by never having smoked. The BBC marked his sixtieth birthday by scheduling a special 'John Peel Night' in his honour. 'I may be sixty and fat,' he told listeners to his show that week, 'but the music will be good,' he promised, as though we didn't know that yet.

In July 1998, John was invited to curate the line-up for that year's Meltdown concerts at London's Festival

Hall. Peel filled the week-long run of shows with a predictably motley crew, including thrash-poppers Magoo, the always eccentric Gorky's Zygotic Mynci, and the drably exotic Cornershop. John interspersed his onstage introductions with regular reference to the then ongoing World Cup, and made sure that all the major games were being broadcast concurrently on a giant video screen in the foyer, with the second night's concert postponed while England's game against Argentina reached its agonising climax in Saint-Etienne, the match in which a twenty-two-year-old David Beckham would fatally damage England's chances by needlessly getting sent off.

CHAPTER FOUR

The Home Team

Nineteen Ninety-Eight was also the year John was invited to become the presenter of a new Radio 4 programme to be called *Home Truths*, a programme which seemed to confirm his status as the nation's favourite, slightly eccentric uncle. Unafraid of taking on new challenges, he accepted and the programme quickly earned a reputation for the warmth of its storytelling. Derived from a previous Radio 4 programme called *Offspring* which John had presented for two or three years, the original idea for *Home Truths* was that it should be 'something on children'. But the pilot was rejected and the idea retooled, then resubmitted as the broader programme that would reflect on the trials, tribulations and delights of family life as a whole, from youngest to eldest: a subject close to John's own heart.

Because he wanted to spend the weekends at home, the programme was recorded every Thursday afternoon and broadcast at nine o'clock on Saturday morning. Writing all his own scripts for the programme, given the format, he became even more famous for slipping in true-life anecdotes about his own family. At one point the children objected, particularly youngest daughter, Flossie, so John agreed to cut down on the references, if not eradicate them completely. As he told Radio 4's *Live Chat* programme in 2001: 'I don't refer to them as much as I once did, because it started to intrude on their lives a bit. So they let me know they didn't like it much. It's the same for anybody who has a public job, it can colour your relationship with your children. Because they're embarrassed by you. The response we get is usually affectionate. People say: "You must be Sheila, we've heard so much about you."'

If it seemed an incongruous move for the rebel music master of Radio 1 to make, John said he hoped 'there'd be some kind of cross-fertilisation. I'd like people who listen to Radio 4 to listen to Radio 1 and vice versa.' Certainly his lively, off-the-cuff remarks put some crackle into Radio 4 listeners' Saturday mornings. On one early programme, during a discussion about the pros and cons of having a Scandinavian wife, John commented wryly: 'There was a time at Radio 1 where I think I was the only DJ who *didn't* have a Scandinavian wife!'

There was also a brief furore over the edition, in February 2003, when John hoped to interview Steve Gough, a nude rights campaigner – but was thwarted when Gough was prevented from entering BBC studios in Southampton naked. Forty-three-year-old Mr Gough had already cycled naked in the winter rain from his Eastleigh home five miles away to do the interview and was said to be very disappointed, not to mention very cold, when he was forced to cycle all the way back again without at least the warmth of knowing he had been on the show. John was sympathetic but there didn't seem much he could actually do. Certainly he wasn't about to risk the sanity of the *Home Truths* production staff by taking off his own clothes in protest.

Mainly, the show focused on more serious stories. Managing to avoid falling into mawkishness, John's uncanny ability to put other people at their ease immediately defined his style on the show: part confessional, part anecdotal, drawing humorous, quirky and sometimes tragically sad stories out of listeners without sensationalising. As John said, 'I'm not Jeremy Paxman.'

When John agreed to present the programme, he did so on the condition that it would be free from the usual rent-a-celebs and focused instead on true-life stories from real people. John Walters, who had pursued his own successful career as a broadcaster after leaving Radio 1, would sit in occasionally for John on the show, before his death in July 2001. In characteristically glib but unerringly accurate fashion, Walters described the show as being 'about people who had fridges called Renfrewshire.'

Writing and presenting the Radio 4 programme was

much harder work than assembling his Radio 1 shows, which featured meticulous running orders but largely improvisational links. And for all its plaudits, he conceded in private, there were times when even he thought the show didn't work. 'You think, oh god, I wish I hadn't said that.' The similarity between his Radio 1 and Radio 4 programmes was, he said, his liking for 'mixing things up', which explained how such disparate items as a family tragedy and an item on toenail clippings might end up on the same programme. 'It's the same with the music on the Radio 1 programmes,' he said. 'Having some kind of banjo thing, then going straight into drum'n'bass.'

Of the many hundreds of editions of *Home Truths* that John wrote and presented, a typical example was 'Father's Secret', the story of Frank, who was brought up by his mother but, at fifty-seven, had only the faintest notion of who his father was – other than his name, Richard Craig-Hallam, and that he had presided over the Japanese war crimes tribunal following the Second World War. After his mother's death in 1991, Frank began to research his father's history in earnest, discovering what turned out to be a rich history – plus an introduction to a whole new family he never knew he had. As John observed, 'Everybody has something about themselves that others would find completely bizarre.'

Another item, headed 'Letters From Zanzibar',

concerned the story of Elizabeth Smith, who left her hometown of Thirsk in North Yorkshire, in 1863, to travel to India to marry her fiancé Henry Jacob. Henry had left England four years before to work as a book-keeper for a steam navigation company. Happily, it was a successful marriage, and Elizabeth wrote several letters home over the years describing her life overseas. When the letters were unearthed over a hundred years later by her great-great-niece, Yvonne Bird, the *Home Truths* teams invited her into the studio to read from them, beginning with the actual letter Henry had penned to Elizabeth's father, asking for her hand. The collected letters were later published as the book, *A Quaker Family in India and Zanzibar 1863–1865 (Letters from Elizabeth and Henry Jacob)*, edited by Yvonne Bird.

Equally poignant, but in an entirely different way, was 'Lost Birth Certificate', the strange story of Laura, who lost her birth certificate twelve years ago and has never been able to replace it, despite years of trying. As a result, Laura no longer officially exists, and therefore can't get access to passport, credit cards, loans or any of the other myriad ways in which we need ID these days.

There were also more offbeat stories, like the one titled 'Holy Communion', about Georgina and her daughter Savannah. When Savannah took her First Holy Communion in 2004, her mother treated her to a 'fairy tale' celebration with, at enormous expense, a

Cinderella-style glass coach drawn by two white horses. John began the interview by asking simply, 'Why?' Or, even more intriguing, 'Skips', the story of Jan and her lifelong obsession with other people's skips – and her inability to resist rummaging around in them and rescuing the things people throw out. Her husband John, once disdainful of this practice, had thrown in the towel long ago and now joined in with her.

Speaking in an online interview with *Reader's Digest*, John said: 'Interviewees are not especially grateful when you speak to them in overly reverential tones. I have often found that if you can introduce a moment of discreet insensitivity (if you see what I mean) it releases a sort of emotional safety valve.' The hardest interview he had done up till then was with a woman from Chesterfield whose son had died in an accident as they awaited his A level results. 'At the same time, our Thomas was also waiting to hear his,' John recalled. 'The interviewee was fantastic and ended up having to console me, as I had to keep stopping the recording because I was crying.'

Chris Berthoud, who led the original team that produced *Home Truths*, said: 'John was an exceptionally talented presenter, and one of the nicest men I've ever met. I don't think I've ever laughed so much as when I was with John – nor have I ever been so impressed by a person's handling of extremely sensitive interviews. We stayed in touch after I left the programme and when I last saw him at his sixty-fifth birthday party he was at the top of his game, advising guests on which red wine to drink and explaining the relative merits of the two bands which played that night.'

The programme was not without its critics, of course. Journalist and broadcaster Janet Street-Porter was the first to air her 'hatred' of *Home Truths*, finding its style too smug and 'Middle-England'. Even John's old pal Andy Kershaw admitted he didn't like his new show, going so far as to describe it as 'cloying, sentimental and indulgent'. While Gillian Reynolds wrote in the *Telegraph*: 'I couldn't abide *Home Truths*. I didn't like to hear the old lion tamed; the wizard of hippiedom weaving sentimental spells for the suburbs.' Although she did concede: 'How often do you get someone who has lived a bit, laughed a lot, known all the major names in rock and discovered quite a few of them, settling down for an hour on a Saturday morning to listen to the nation's phobias – and be genuinely, constructively interested?'

Certainly the one and a half million listeners the programme attracted each week – an enormous audience for Radio 4, let alone early on a Saturday morning – had few complaints. Nor did the vast majority of the critics, and in 1999 *Home Truths* would garner no fewer than four Sony Radio awards.

On Thursday, 26 November 1998, the same year

Home Truths began broadcasting, John was 'staggered' but 'deeply honoured' to be awarded an OBE. He travelled down to London with Sheila and all the children, plus his brothers, Alan and Frank. Only Sheila was allowed to accompany him into Buckingham Palace, where he received his award from HRH The Prince of Wales.

Original *Home Truths* producer Chris Berthoud was waiting outside the palace gates as John and Sheila emerged to meet the children. It had been an 'interesting experience,' said a still flushed Peel. 'A bit like going to a church service in a church to which you don't belong. The band plays continually and not especially well. I don't want to be unkind [but] they seemed to be playing Songs from the Shows, "Those You Have Loved",' he joked. There was one thing, though, that the Palace band 'got spectacularly right. There was a man who was being awarded the MBE for his services to the River Thames, and as his name was called they went into "Jolly Boating Weather"!'

Known for dressing casually, on this occasion he had deigned to wear a suit – originally bought for Sheila's father's funeral, he confessed. The bright red tie he also wore was, of course, his 'tribute to Liverpool Football Club, though they scarcely deserve it! I was hoping [Charles] would ask about that, but he didn't.'

John had also requested that he be given the honour in the family name of Ravenscroft. 'They'd got me down as Peel,' he explained, 'but today I wanted to be Ravenscroft for the sake of the family.' He also had to remember various manoeuvres as he went up to meet the Prince. 'When you've spoken to him, and he shakes your hand, which is the signal that it's all over, kid, you have to back away, then bow slightly, turn to the right, then away.' He managed it, though. 'We were all very proud of him,' smiled Sheila.

When, just eighteen months later, Andy Kershaw was sacked from Radio 1, to be replaced by yet another dance music programme, Peel was understandably devastated and all the old paranoia about his own 'tenuous' position temporarily returned. Fortunately, Kershaw, recipient of four Sony Radio awards during his fifteen-year tenure at the station, was soon picked up by Radio 3, whose Controller Roger Wright told him that what he most enjoyed about Andy's Radio 1 show was that he never knew what was coming next – a trick the apprentice had surely learned from the old master.

Meanwhile, the Peel antennae continued to twitch unstoppably. The Strokes, a new American band signed to Rough Trade, also 'arrived' with their first Peel session, in June 2001, blasting out tracks from their first EP, *The Modern Age*, and suddenly sounding like it. Six months later their debut album, *Is This It*, was a huge hit all over the world. A month after the Strokes session, Peel had another new American band called the White Stripes doing their first session for him. 'Hotel

Yorba' most sticks in my mind from this session, though what most people now recall, of course, is how it lit the blue touch paper for the band, starting the media avalanche that would turn them into the biggest, most influential rock band of the new millennium.

John had first heard the White Stripes, fronted by a supposed brother-and-sister act (in reality a separated couple) by the name of Jack and Meg White, when he bought their first eponymously titled album on US import from a small shop in the Netherlands. 'I just liked the look of it,' he shrugged. 'You develop an instinct.' After their first session for the show, breaking his rule about no longer fraternising with the guests, John took the penniless pair out for dinner at a nearby Thai restaurant. Later, it looked as if there might be a Bolan-like falling-out in store. It was thankfully avoided, but only just. The problem: when John was sent an early pre-release copy of *Elephant* by the band personally, he proceeded to play most of it on his show that night. The band's US record label, V2, went berserk – convinced the home-tapers and internet freaks would have a field day (which they probably did, not that it stopped the album going on to become a multimillion seller). John found himself on the end of a severe dressing-down over the transatlantic phone line. He was so upset that for a long while afterwards he made a point of sending any mail from their UK label, XL, back to them unopened.

John was also doing more live gigs again. His last appearance in a serious dance club (festivals aside) had been in Manchester's Hacienda in 1991. 'I was stuck in some back room and people would occasionally stick their head round, then wander off looking very disappointed,' he recalled. Now, eleven years later, he was back – and not just anywhere but at one of the most fashionable new clubs in London – Fabric.

'Nowadays,' he said, shorn of the Roadshow title but still wielding an overflowing Box of Records, 'I "play out" (as the young people say) once or twice a year.' He wept at the climax of his first set at the club in February 2002, as the crowd chanted his name. 'I was very, very nervous,' he said afterwards. 'I don't do this kind of thing often, I had no idea what to expect. But the crowd were wonderful.' He was particularly moved by the fact that people were still singing 'Teenage Kicks' long after the set had finished. 'When the offer came from Fabric, I mentioned it to the people at Radio 1 and they said it was a good idea,' he explained. Then he added ruefully, 'Mainly, I imagine, so they could get free tickets.'

John played again at Fabric in the summer of 2002, getting such an overwhelming response that the club asked him to compile one of its monthly mix CDs, another first for the venerable broadcaster, who chose only tracks from records 'currently in the Box'. Titled *FabricLive.07: John Peel*, and released in December 2002, the album featured everything from drum'n'bass to northern soul to a hillbilly cover of Iggy Pop's 'Lust For Life'. A DJ mix album, it would be fair to say, completely unlike any other before.

That didn't mean that John was about to start chomping E, wearing tinted wraparound sunglasses and being reborn as a dance DJ. In fact, John was increasingly anti-drugs as he grew older. How to give his own children the best advice on the subject, he said, was a subject that had vexed him. 'It was a difficult thing to work out, given that they would almost certainly have drug experiences, as I did myself – although I'm more of a red wine man now. I told them that their greatest danger lay in the lack of quality control, that they couldn't really know what they were buying and therefore couldn't know what effect the drugs would have on them.'

Mojo editor-in-chief Phil Alexander first got to know John in the late nineties, when he was the co-presenter of Radio 1's weekly *Rock Show*, which used to follow the Peel show onto air at midnight every Tuesday. 'Mary Anne Hobbs used to be the main presenter of the show, I was just someone for her to banter with and join in whenever we had guests on the show like Lemmy or whoever, and I wouldn't usually make an appearance for the first half-hour. Nevertheless, I was expected to be ready at my post by the time the show started. However, due to an inherent ability to rarely be on time for anything, I was nearly always running late by the time I arrived at the studios each Tuesday.

'One particular night, I arrived to the sound of booming heavy metal coming out of the in-house speakers in reception and I immediately panicked. I couldn't be so late, could I, that I'd completely missed the start of the show? I legged it up to the studio and arrived just in time to hear John back-announcing the record – some industrial-strength little ditty from Morbid Angel, as I recall – and realised my mistake. When I later told John about it in passing, he found it so funny he began ending all his Tuesday night shows with some outrageous example of extreme metal noise – I seem to recall the name Bolt Thrower coming up once or twice. For me, the joke wore a little thin after the first two or three times – mainly because it nearly always caught me out. But for John it remained a constant source of chucklesome amusement.'

Alexander says his most cherished memory of Peel was when – in his previous incarnation as head-honcho at *Kerrang!* magazine – he persuaded the DJ to present an award at the televised annual *Kerrang!* Awards, in 2001.

'Although I knew he had been obliged to take part in various Radio 1 and BBC awards shows over the years, I also knew from speaking with him that John hated the very idea of awards shows,' says Phil now. 'But in this particular case, the award I wanted to present was called the Spirit of Independence Award –

commemorating a group or individual on their outstanding services to indie music, in one way or another. That year the recipients were to be Napalm Death, the Birmingham-based band whose speciality in their earliest days had been these excessively brief blasts of extreme metal noise, lasting sometimes as little as twenty or thirty seconds. Needless to say this made them virtually unplayable by pretty much all conventional radio standards. Equally needless to say, John had been the only DJ in Britain to give them exposure.

'Because of this background, I hoped I might be able to persuade John, against his better nature, to actually present them with the award. True to form, he agreed immediately, saying that he would be "deeply honoured", in fact.

'Come the big occasion, I had expected him to have something interesting to say when he took to the stage because John was one of those rare people who always seemed to have something interesting to say about pretty much everything, even if it was just to inform you he really knew nothing about it. What I hadn't anticipated, however, was that he would give one of the most memorable performances of any guest award presenter I think we've ever had.'

The masked US metal group, Slipknot, who had just broken into the charts for the first time that year, were busy trying to draw attention to themselves by wreaking havoc in the corner of the room in which they and their table of guests had been seated.

'It wasn't the normal sort of food-throwing shenanigans,' says Alexander. 'They were heckling the guests and attempting to destroy furniture. This was all going on as John took to the stage to present the Spirit of Independence award to Napalm Death – and he just lost it with them. It was fantastic! Quite unexpected but utterly brilliant! He just looked witheringly over to where all this carnage was going on and said: "Will you just shut up." It just stopped them dead. I can't remember verbatim what he said next but it ran along the lines of: "I'm about to turn sixty-two next birthday, and therefore I'm allowed to ramble on a bit. So can I just say I never expected to be sharing the same room with a bunch of retarded rednecks from the middle of fucking nowhere."

'It was just the most amazing moment, especially considering the award he was about to present and to who – Napalm Death, without whom a band like Slipknot might still be prancing around in spandex. The really interesting thing was that Slipknot immediately stopped what they were doing and sat down nicely at their table again. It said a lot about John: how accepting he was of true innovators like Napalm Death, but how the Slipknot level of stupidity was not the kind he would have any truck with.'

Alexander also fondly recalled John guest-hosting

the Radio 1 Breakfast Show one week, in the wake of the sudden departure of broadcasting *enfant terrible* Chris Evans. 'I remember John played something by Aphex Twin at about 8.15 one morning – this stunningly relentless, one-beat drone that sounded totally strange at that time of the morning. You could imagine a nation of mums and dads bashing radios with their fists, assuming there must be something wrong with the signal. Even I nearly choked on my cornflakes...'

When Simon Garfield interviewed John extensively for his 1998 book, *The Nation's Favourite: True Adventures of Radio 1*, his main impression as they shared endless bottles of rioja was of 'a hugely sensitive man who cared very much about his music and his family, but also about how he was regarded by others.'

He recalled Peel telling him: 'A lot of people working [at Radio 1] come up to me and make rather un-British little speeches about how they grew up listening to my programme, which is lovely to hear, and then you can think to yourself, "Well, perhaps you wouldn't even be working here if it wasn't for me," and I quite like the thought of that. But even the younger ones stopped listening to the programme at some stage. It seems that people listen to the programme for a while and then stop, and often listen to the programme later on in their lives.' Sometimes younger listeners wrote in to say, 'I was listening to your programme in my bedroom the other night when I was doing my homework, and my mum came in and said, "What are you listening to?" I said, "John Peel," and she said, "Oh, I used to listen to him when I was your age."' John added: 'It's nice being woven into people's lives in that way.'

In 2001, more than six thousand people voted in a *Radio Times* poll which saw the now sixty-two-year-old Peel beating all his younger Radio 1 colleagues to triumph as one of the the most attractive voices on BBC Radio, coming fourth best overall behind, in descending order, Terry Wogan (Radio 2), Peter Donaldson (Radio 4), and Brian Perkins (Radio 4). No other Radio 1 DJ made the Top 10.

In latter years, the famously flat but well-rounded Peel voice could be heard narrating television documentaries on such quintessentially British subjects as the Lancaster bomber and British road transport. He also wrote and presented *Sounds of the Suburbs*, a series in which Peel travelled round Britain examining pockets of the country and the music that sprang out of them. In more recent years, he could also be found contributing to BBC 2's humorous look at the irritations of modern life, *Grumpy Old Men*. And he was once famously forced to climb into a pram and be a 'bearded baby' at the climax of one of Vic Reeves and Bob Mortimer's *Shooting Stars* shows, the week he was a guest. Asked once why he hadn't got rid of the beard at the same time he ditched all his other pre-punk accoutrements, he replied that without it he looked like 'a cross between his mum and the Italian dictator Benito Mussolini.'

John was also in demand as a voice-over artist for television documentaries, such as BBC 1's *A Life Of Grime*, which introduced the incorrigible Mr Trebus character – and several treacly voice-overs for TV ads (including narrating the Andrex puppy ads, and Pampers nappy ads), though he reportedly refused to work on adverts for products that he didn't actually favour himself. He also did a column for *Radio Times* in recent years, weekly musings on whatever took his fancy, a grown-up relative of the old *Sounds* column, minus the scantily clad schoolgirls, sadly.

His manager and long-time friend Clive Selwood said, 'He never compromised on his personal life or his musical tastes, and what you saw was what you got.' He added: 'Most DJs have only seen Radio 1 as a stepping stone to hosting a quiz show on TV and, while John has been offered hundreds of quiz shows, he prefers to sit in a darkened studio, relating how he feels to the audience.'

Fame – real fame – was never Peel's game. 'I have a photograph of myself with the DJ Jeff Mills,' he once said. 'I look like some dodgy European businessman who's found himself a cute Malaysian boy for the night. I keep it close to my side as a reminder of what I really look like.'

John also, despite his fear of flying, broadened his travels in more recent years, visiting eastern Europe for the first time in 2001 and journeying all the way to New Zealand in 2002, where, in the company of the novelist Andrew O'Hagan he was part of a delegation there to 'represent British culture' – an assignment John viewed with some bemusement. 'I have to say I've never fallen into camaraderie with someone so quickly in my life,' O'Hagan later recalled. The first night, the writer joined John and Sheila for dinner at – inevitably – an Indian restaurant. 'I realised John and Sheila were one of the very few couples whose relationship I envied: she loved his jokes, and he just thought there was nothing in the world to match her.'

The next day, waiting to meet a delegation of Maori dignitaries, O'Hagan was discussing the band the Wedding Present with John when 'I broke off and said something nice to him about Sheila. His eyes filled up and he lost his words. "Thank you, Andrew," he said eventually. "I think that, too."' Everywhere they went people would present him with tapes, records and CDs. 'By day three, he had ninety-two of them.'

John was equally well loved in the Suffolk village of Great Finborough where he lived, and well-known to all the locals at his village pub, the Chestnut Horse, just a mile from his home. Mother-of-three Alison Jones, who used to babysit Peel's children, said: 'He had a real sense of belonging to this community. He would just go to the pub and be himself.' Neighbour and poultry factory worker Robin Fisher added: 'He was a great bloke and always had time for a chat. He used to run the local youth club when I was a teenager and took around twenty of us away on holidays. He was famous – but it didn't make any difference to us.'

John once said: 'Perhaps the reason people put up with me is that I don't pretend to be anything other than what I am – an overweight sixty-something with four children and a sore back.' He meant it about the sore back, too, as he never tired of reminding listeners and colleagues alike. He had been reaching down to pick a CD up from the floor when 'I turned round and something snapped.' He visited an osteopath several times but the problem never really went away.

John also had other, less talked about health concerns. He had been diagnosed as suffering from diabetes in September 2001. For the rest of his life, John would have to inject himself daily with insulin – which he claimed made him grumpy in the mornings because of his low blood sugar – and try and keep to more strict meal times. Easy to say, not always easy to accomplish when you worked strange hours and did so much slogging back and forth on the motorway.

Over the last couple of years of his career, some industry insiders half expected Peel to join the exodus to Radio 2, in the wake of the station's revamped new look, with the addition of people like Bob Harris,

Johnnie Walker, Mark Radcliffe, Paul Gambaccini and Simon Mayo. But John was not convinced. 'I may be old but the programme isn't. I think what I do belongs on Radio 1,' he said, defiant to the end.

In 2002, he received the broadcasting industry's highest accolade, the Sony Gold Award, marking his outstanding contribution to radio over thirty-five years. He also earned a place that year in the Radio Academy Hall of Fame. Over the years, he was also awarded a host of honorary degrees – from Liverpool University, the Open University, Portsmouth University, Bradford University and the University of East Anglia – plus doctorates from the Polytechnic University of East Anglia and Sheffield Hallam University, and a Fellowship from John Moores University, Liverpool.

Also in 2002, he came an astonishing forty-third in the BBC's 100 Greatest Britons poll. Coming not far below such esteemed historical figures as Winston Churchill, Captain Cook, Guy Fawkes and John Lennon, he was amazed to find himself ahead of Sir Walter Raleigh, J.R.R. Tolkien and the Unknown Soldier. 'It's quite clearly bollocks,' John said. 'But in a way, quite gratifying bollocks. When they invited me in for an interview about it, I suspected it was a piss-take. I thought someone would leap out and say, "You arrogant bastard."'

Whether he felt entirely comfortable with the

description or not, John Peel had become a national institution. Although he never actually went to university and would characteristically play down his later achievements (he was once admonished by a teacher from Huddersfield who wrote in to complain that he was discouraging people from going to college), behind closed doors John was inordinately proud of all his honours. He always enjoyed attending the various ceremonies. It was nice, he said, to 'dress up in silly clothes and be important for a few hours.' He liked to joke at his gigs about being a doctor now and therefore, should anyone feel poorly throughout the night, he could be relied on to come and loosen their clothes.

Ultimately, he said when the joshing stopped, he took more pride in the fact that his Radio 1 shows still had the highest percentage of listeners under the age of sixteen on the station. All the more astounding as he never made any effort to appear 'young'. 'Kids aren't as dumb as radio and television people think they are,' he said. 'They'd sooner have somebody my age being straight with them than somebody who's thirty pretending to be eighteen.' If he had to choose between doing his music programme and *Home Truths*, 'I'd do the music programmes every time – that's when I kind of come alive.'

His only regret, he said, was that he would like to have been taller 'and have more hair and a bigger willy', but apart from that he had 'the perfect life, really'.

'People say my self-deprecatory manner is starting to look like conceit, but you can't get out of that,' he said with a shrug. He still called Tony Blackburn – winner of the inaugural *I'm A Celebrity – Get Me Out of Here*, in 2002 – an 'amiable buffoon'. Though after all these years, he admitted that he did, in fact, nurse a grudging respect for his old Radio 1 nemesis. 'He's remained true to what he believes in, in the same way I have.'

With all four children now grown up and either attending university or just having left it, the only blot on his personal horizon, he claimed, was the latter-day state of Liverpool FC, who only ever seemed to beat old rivals Manchester United these days – and nobody else of any significance. But then the modern game had become 'distorted', he complained, by the massive injections of television money it had begun getting in the nineties. 'The rich get richer and the poor get poorer, so it's very undemocratic.'

Over the last year of his life, John shared a large open-plan office at Radio 1 where all the 'specialist' DJs worked, called G12. A large ground-floor office where the headphones-only rule was abandoned after six p.m., it buzzed with rock music from Zane Lowe's side of the room, drum'n'bass from Fabio and Grooverider, while all sorts of ambient vibes would be emanating from Annie Nightingale's corner. Before his shows he would often take his team out for a curry and a glass or two of red wine, before returning to G12. Peel would choose the wine in a paternal manner, sniffing the sampler in his glass before pronouncing it to be acceptable. Then it was down to the basement to broadcast his show live from his favourite studio Y1.

As he sat there with his headphones on, listening to music and opening envelopes in which even more music waited to be played, he told colleagues and anyone else within earshot, he just wanted to hear 'something that I can't relate to anything else. It happened with Roxy Music. It happened with the Smiths. You couldn't tell what the Smiths were listening to. And, of course, with the contemporary kind of electronica, a lot of that stuff you can't really tell where that's come from either. And that's quite good, I think. That's quite healthy.'

John pointed out that while people always praise him for having kept up with modern music, he himself felt he had not changed at all from the callow youth with the slightly suspect, prototype mullet who first began mumbling on air late at night for Radio London. He said he felt that what he did now was 'essentially the same' as he'd always done. He laughingly added that he even still played vinyl records ... despite the modern radio system being run on computerised hard disk, he still liked to use turntables 'as much as possible'. He simply liked 'the sound of vinyl better, it's a kind of warmer sound.'

On the whole, he thought, Radio 1 in the twenty-first century was a 'huge improvement' on the bland edifice he had helped to chip away at so stoically for most of his career. There were 'many more DJs that are actually interested in music than when Radio 1 started.' One recent session he loved a lot was by the reggae band Culture. I recall hearing him describing on air how the Culture session later released on album was 'one of my top ten sessions of all time, I think.' I wondered how many hundreds of times I had heard him say it before. Meaning it every time, too, the way you always knew John did.

In recent years, John most enjoyed broadcasting from Peel Acres, where the Pig, and sometimes daughter Flossie, were able to help out on the show. Joey Burns of Calexico, one of the new groups that Peel had recently championed, recalls going up to the house in Suffolk to record a Peel session last year: 'We were fortunate enough to get to play at his house, with his wife Sheila and the family there. We were pretty amazed that anyone would be happy with musicians tramping through the mud and setting up equipment, but they were so comfortable and so courteous.'

Studio sessions were usually four tracks recorded and mixed in a single day, giving them that rough, demo-like feel that John prized, somewhere between a live performance and a finished recording; the sessions from Peel Acres, however, were broadcast live. One hugely memorable example of more recent times was the one Polly Harvey did for him in the summer of 2004.

Proving again that it was not true that John – who had been the first DJ to play PJ Harvey songs ten years before – abandoned artists once they became successful. As long as the music was still there, so was John.

But although his on-air tastes remained as periodically outlandish as ever, at home visitors were more likely to be treated to some old-style blues as he uncorked the rioja. John also broke with a lifetime's habit and played a few more older records on his show towards the end of his career, specifically in a new section he dubbed 'The Pig's Big 78' – in which he played a 78 rpm record chosen by Sheila. In addition to *Home Truths* and his Radio 1 show – now broadcast three nights a week, Tuesday to Thursday – for many years John had also done a special show for the BBC World Service, as well as his own weekly show on the British Forces Broadcasting Service (BFBS) which had been going for over thirty years, plus regular shows for VPRO Radio 3 in the Netherlands and Radio Eins in Germany.

All his professional life, John had endeavoured to 'look a little further ahead'. Now, with the arrival of the internet and modern satellite and digital communications, more people than ever listened to the show from around the world. Even more people sent records, to the point where the programme had become more of a global event in recent times, taking on a slightly more 'interactive' feel. All of which only made

John happier to still be spinning the discs. 'It's great when you get a response on a record from Nigeria, as it's just going out.'

Even towards the end of his life, after more than forty years of recognition, John would still register surprise whenever he was recognised in public, which was often. 'I really am someone who just got lucky,' he once said. 'A guy who drifted into a position I used to think would be the job of my dreams.' He even had a record named after him in 2003 when the outfit CLSM released a single called 'John Peel is Not Enough'. John was so delighted that not only did he play it on his show several times, but he dedicated an entire show to happy hardcore tracks, in the vain hope that it might spawn its own show.

In September 2004, John claimed he was still in mourning for the recent loss of his favourite car for many years, a Mercedes 190. After putting in more than half a million miles on the clock, he had finally agreed to the now decrepit old girl being carted off to the scrapyard. To avoid any unseemly display of emotion, he said, he had made sure he was away in London when the dreadful deed was done.

He wasn't sad for long, however, swiftly replacing it with a 'tyre-scalding' 3.2-litre Alfa Romeo 147, which he laughingly described as 'an old man's last raging against the dying of the light'. In a nod to the environmental concerns of his family and neighbours, he had also recently purchased a hybrid petrol-electric Toyota Prius. 'We took the Prius on our annual trip to Barcelona,' he told the *Sunday Telegraph*. 'It's amazing how much money you save: we got there on about ten pounds' worth of petrol.' Naturally, the new Prius, like all John's cars, was also home to hundreds of cassettes and CDs. 'I've always imagined I'd die by driving into the back of a truck while trying to read the name on a cassette, and people would say, "He would have wanted to go that way." Well, I want them to know that I wouldn't…'

In March 2003, when news was announced that John had signed a deal with the publishers Transworld to write his autobiography, the size of the advance he reportedly received – a package said to be in excess of £1.5 million – sent shock waves throughout the publishing industry. It was one of biggest sums ever paid in Britain for a celebrity memoir, beating recent advances reportedly paid to the likes of Murray Walker (£1.4 million), Sir Alex Ferguson (£1.2 million), Geri Halliwell (£500,000) and Billy Connolly (£250,000). 'It's an absolutely staggering sum,' said one prominent publisher. 'Peel is a very nice guy but I am not sure that what he's got to say is worth that much.'

Amongst celebrities, only David Beckham, who reportedly agreed an advance of more than £2 million for his autobiography with HarperCollins in 2002, is thought to have pulled off a better deal. In fact, the price had become inflated partly due to the fierce bidding war that broke out amongst London publishers once it became known Peel's memoirs were up for grabs, his reputation for honesty being the main drawing card, according to one well-known London literary agent in the pop field. As such, the outline that was sent to prospective publishers included promising disclosures about his early life, his troubles at Shrewsbury as an adolescent, and of course his tangled love life and intermittent drug-taking throughout the sixties and early seventies, plus expectedly lurid never-before-told tales of Marc, Bowie, Rod, et al. Plus the full story behind his ill-conceived marriage to Shirley.

Cat Ledger, John's literary agent, was said to have begun the bidding by asking for at least £1 million – and immediately attracted instant offers from half a dozen publishers. Patrick Janson-Smith, joint managing director of Transworld, winners of the bidding war, said he was confident Peel's book would be a big success and justify such a large advance.

'John Peel is a much-loved and much-admired figure and there is a real story there. As a DJ, he's been at the centre of the cultural scene since the 1960s and now he has a very strong appeal to Middle England through *Home Truths*. People absolutely love the programme.' He predicted that Transworld would recover the advance with hardback sales of 300,000 to 400,000 and similar paperback figures.

Eighteen months later, with a deadline of March 2005 looming for his manuscript, John admitted privately that he hadn't got very far with writing his book yet, blaming his difficulties in part on having to use a computer, which had sapped him of his energy. Then, once he did get going, he accidentally deleted the first 5,000 words and had to start again. The children had helped out, though, and by the time he went on holiday with Sheila in October 2004, he was said to have written a large proportion of the section dealing with his childhood, with various sidetracks into his early years in the music business.

He had decided the book would not adhere to a strict chronological order, he said, because that was 'rather tedious'. Instead, he intended the story to spool backwards and forwards. And he had decided that the book would be dedicated to his old housemaster at Shrewsbury, R.H.J. Brooke.

Whenever he wasn't working, he sped back home to Sheila. He would rather spend a day at home with his wife and children, his chickens, cats and dogs, than do anything else. Except, of course, for those times when he found himself wandering outside to one of the sheds and poking through the records and tapes, the detritus of his long playing life, still looking for something he couldn't quite manage to find apparently.

One thing Peel Acres was not, despite the visiting bands and in-house studio, was rock'n'roll. It was never meant to be. One of the reasons John felt he had survived so long was because of his conspicuous absence from the sort of shallow showbiz get-togethers that have always engulfed most high-profile DJs. He liked to boast that he couldn't remember the last time he had attended a showbiz party, and claimed he hadn't visited the offices of a major record company in more than twenty-five years.

'We keep ourselves to ourselves,' he said, 'and I have to say the world is very happy to cooperate with this. People aren't constantly trying to lure us out. It's not like: "Mick's on the phone again"; "Oh, God, tell him I'm in the bath."'

More than anything, he said in September 2004, he was just looking forward to going on holiday with Sheila. She needed a break and he had arranged for them to go to Peru – a country they had both long dreamed of visiting.

CHAPTER FIVE

... So Hard To Beat

On the occasion of his sixtieth birthday, John Peel had joked: 'I would quite like to die on the air, but not in a kind of melodramatic way. I would prefer to go during a long track. Then a continuity announcer would come on, trying to stay calm and saying, "John seems to have been taken ill. We will take you over to Radio Two." Then you would hear the sound of my heels being dragged down the steps and that will be that.' Acknowledging the fact that his family had a history of early death, he had added: 'By that reckoning, I've only got about seven or eight years left.'

Not that John was ready to follow his old friend, John Walters, into retirement. By the time he had reached his sixty-fifth birthday, in August 2004, John was still defiantly pooh-poohing any suggestion that he might himself be coming to the end of the road. 'I don't plan to retire before I die,' he said. 'I don't even like the idea of retirement. I don't want to play golf. I just want to keep doing what I'm doing. I do regard the playing of golf as like entering the antechamber to death. When my mates tell me they've started playing golf, I mentally cross them off the Christmas card list.'

John did not get his wish about dying on air. In the end, however, he died doing as he had done, for so many years of his life: not playing golf, swapping matey DJ banter with the chaps at the 19th hole, but out there still looking for 'something I haven't heard before,' his beloved wife, Sheila, by his side, and a glass of decent red to hand.

In an interview with the *Sunday Telegraph* in May 2004, John had been invited to discuss his favourite holiday destinations for a piece in their Travel section. He listed his honeymoon trip to Egypt in 1974 as probably his best holiday ever, but also mentioned a family holiday in 2003 staying at a charming old château in the Dordogne. Asked where he might like to go to next if he could choose anywhere, John instantly replied: 'South America, for new cultural experiences. But there's so much to see that it's rather daunting.'

He went on to explain how, despite making an excellent overall recovery from her brain haemorrhage, Sheila's eyesight was now starting to deteriorate quite seriously and therefore he wanted her to see as many sights as possible while she was still able to fully enjoy them. Sheila's mother had also recently died, and her father, himself no longer in the best of health, had moved into the family home in Suffolk with them. This year had also seen the thirtieth anniversary of their wedding, and with all the children now in various stages of readiness to fly the coop,

John badly wanted to give Sheila a much-needed holiday.

When the newspaper's travel section editors read what John had said, they came up with the idea of inviting Peel to write an article for them about his 'dream trip' to South America. They felt his 'first-timer' point of view, coupled to his innate sense of curiosity and droll sense of humour would probably make for a fascinating piece. When the *Telegraph* editors sounded him out about where, in particular, in South America he would most like to go, he discussed it with Sheila and they both chose Peru.

'I've got a bad back and diabetes,' John warned them. 'I'm not the most robust of travellers. But I would like to see as much of the country as I can.' He asked for recommendations of the sights he and Sheila should try and see and was told about highlights such as Cuzco and the ancient Incan ruins of Machu Picchu, the famous Lake Titicaca, the spectacular Colca Canyon and several other prime locations. They were all dutifully placed on a proposed itinerary for the couple to consider, along with several other suggestions for what John was now officially referring to as a 'working holiday'.

With the aid of tour operators Cox & Kings, whose reputation for putting together Latin American tours is well established, John and Sheila eventually whittled it down to three possible options. The first two, on paper, looked like the easiest, in terms of time actually spent travelling. But they also involved a great many internal flights and John, who claimed he would already have to dose himself up with 'a prodigious quantity of tranquillisers' just to get through the fourteen-hour flight from London, was sceptical of his ability to face getting on a plane with such frightening regularity, the little he knew of Latin American domestic airlines not exactly inspiring confidence, either.

In the end, John and Sheila plumped for option three: this would involve a lot more time spent travelling by rail and road, often driving along windy, potholed roads for miles on end. But it only entailed a couple of short domestic flights – with LAN-Peru, the South American airline with the best safety record. The anticipated extra strain on his dodgy back from all the driving, John said, was still infinitely preferable to the thought of spending the entire trip plane-hopping from place to place.

John finally agreed to the trip after phoning the *Telegraph* at the last minute to ask: 'Can I just double-check that you're happy for me to tell it as I see it?' They were and so, their plans finally agreed, John booked a two-week holiday with both his Radio 1 and *Home Truths* production teams, and he and Sheila kissed the family goodbye and set off expectantly from home on the morning of Sunday, 17 October. There had been some confusion at the airport over which flight they were actually booked on to, which only made John's nerves worse, but once they had finally arrived in Lima they began to look forward with excitement to the rest of the trip.

Everything went fairly smoothly to begin with. They spent two nights in Lima, the Peruvian capital, getting over their jet lag and acclimatising to their exotic new surroundings, then moved on to Arequipa, where they were able to catch a spectacular view of the famous giant condors soaring across the cobalt-blue sky above the Colca Canyon. The following day, they rented a car and drove all the way to Puno, known to locals as 'the gateway to Lake Titicaca'. The next day, Friday, still adhering to the tight schedule the *Telegraph* had helped them draw up, John and Sheila caught the train to Cuzco, 350 miles south-east of Lima, where they were booked in for the weekend at the plush Monasterio Hotel.

Their first chance for a proper rest since their arrival in Lima a week before, it was at the hotel in Cuzco that John, restless as ever, put in a phone call to his Radio 1 office in London. Because it was the weekend, he only got through to the office answer-machine, but he left a typically good-humoured and rambling message, asking the team if they would mind using their considerable resources to try and locate the whereabouts of any record shops and/or labels in Cuzco or any of the other stops remaining on the itinerary, as he had not been able to find any himself, despite spending all day Saturday searching the city's crowded markets and back streets. He said if they found any, to ask them kindly to send him some of their records, so that he could take home something he could play on his Radio 1 shows. He said to ask them to address the records to Mr Ravenscroft and drop them off at the hotel. He added, just before putting the phone down, 'Of course, they might just say fuck off and buy your own records ...'

It was the last time any of his Radio 1 colleagues would ever hear from him.

On the Monday, their last day in Cuzco, after another day spent roaming the city sightseeing, John and Sheila had returned to the hotel where they went to their room to relax for a couple of hours before getting ready to go out again for dinner that evening. By eight-thirty, they were sitting together in the hotel lobby bar having pre-dinner drinks. They had been there about half an hour and were just starting to consider where they should eat that night, their last in the old city, when John suddenly stiffened in his seat ... He had suffered what doctors later described as 'a massive coronary attack'. Paramedics were immediately summoned and began administering emergency cardio-pulmonary resuscitation. When that didn't bring immediate results, they stretchered him to the waiting ambulance. Despite their best efforts, John was pronounced dead upon arrival at the hospital.

The doctor who attended John at the scene, Dr Alcides Vargas, told Peruvian radio the next day that the DJ had actually been pronounced dead on the way to the hospital. He speculated that the thin air of the old city – 3,326 metres up in the Andes mountains – may have played a part in triggering the attack.

In shock, Sheila phoned John's brother Alan, and it was he who officially informed the British Embassy in Lima of John's death, at four a.m. local time. The BBC, who Alan called next with the news, agreed to hold back the announcement for a few hours to allow Sheila and Alan to let family, close friends and colleagues know first. It was eventually announced on the Radio 1's midday *Newsbeat* programme on Tuesday, 26 October, followed immediately by blanket announcements across the country on every other radio and TV station, BBC and otherwise. Radio 1 immediately followed the broadcast of the news by playing 'Teenage Kicks'. A nice touch, even if hardly any of us still struggling to absorb the news were actually listening.

To their credit, Radio 1 station chiefs then hastily rearranged the entire day and night's schedule around, as Jo Whiley put it on the lunchtime show, 'more the kind of thing John Peel would like.' Amazingly, for the rest of the day the nation was forced to do without Britney, Christina and the peripatetic Eric Prydz, and were instead assailed by the kinds of records that had been played on daytime so rarely in recent years that they emerged virtually blinking into the light … Joy Division, the Undertones, the Smiths, even the Fall! If there was any public demonstration still needed of just how singular a broadcaster John Peel was, here was the final proof. In life, Peel had been the only person to get these records played on Radio 1. So, too, in death, he proved to be the only person who could get these records played on Radio 1. That night, BBC 3 also paid its respects by displaying in the top left-hand corner of the screen a discreet caption placed next to its logo, proclaiming in elegant white script, 'BBC 3 – dedicated to John Peel'.

In a brief phone interview the day the news of his death was announced, Sheila said John had seemed 'perfectly fine' in the hours leading up to the heart attack. 'We'd been walking around and he was okay until it happened.' They had been looking forward to the next leg of their trip, she said, to see the ancient fortress city of Machu Picchu, before returning to London the following Sunday. Instead, devastated though she was, Sheila was now having to battle with red tape to try to bring his body back. Alan, who had travelled up to the pink-painted house in Great Finborough the same night to be with the children when they got the news, added that it was 'a very sad day'.

John's manager and long-time friend, Clive Selwood,

summed up the feelings of all John's closest friends and family when he said: 'It's a terrible shock. We're absolutely devastated. I've lost a wonderful friend and the world of broadcasting has lost a man who loved music. Sheila is in a terrible way. She has taken it very badly. Sheila has been at the hospital. She wants to bring his body home. I don't know if any of the children are going to fly out but at the moment she is there alone. He suffered a massive heart attack and his life just couldn't be saved.'

Both the Radio 1 and Radio 4 websites were immediately deluged by emails from shocked and distraught Peel listeners. Radio 1 received over five thousand messages from grief-stricken fans the first day alone. One typical message to the BBC News website read as follows: 'Absolutely, genuinely stunned by this sad, sad news. Music radio, and musicians everywhere, owe him a huge debt of gratitude.' Another, older correspondent claimed: 'I feel like a bit of my youth has died with him.' A third emailed: 'A giant of a man, the only true idol I ever had. His loss is immensely saddening.' Yet another added: 'The death of John Peel is a tragic loss to the world of music. In an age of "personality" over ability, vacuous corporate hype, talentless manufactured rubbish and gimmicks, John Peel stayed true to what mattered most in music.' One clearly devastated listener felt moved enough to risk life and limb – not to mention, arrest – by tying a poignant, home-made banner to a walkway over Glasgow's Charing Cross shopping centre, reading simply 'John Peel RIP'.

And, of course, the great and the good of the music world also stopped whatever they were doing to pay tribute to the man who, in so many cases, had firmly kick-started their careers. Famed for the gruff modesty that underpinned his famously laconic style, Peel would doubtless have been embarrassed by the universal expressions of loss, and perhaps even dismissed them in many cases. But that didn't stop the expressions of regret pouring in from all over the world.

Former Undertones singer Feargal Sharkey, now the Government's official live music adviser, led the way when he described Peel as 'the single most important broadcaster we have ever known. I owe everything in my life to John Peel.' He added: 'In the autumn of 1978, something happened that was to change my life for ever – John Peel played "Teenage Kicks" on the radio for the very first time. Today [with the news of his death] it just changed again, for ever.'

Former Undertones bassist Mike Bradley said: '[John] was a very funny, very warm man and we will always be grateful for what he did for the Undertones. Personally, I find it incredible what he did for the band and we always got huge pride out of the fact that he said "Teenage Kicks" was his favourite single. He always had his finger on the pulse of the music industry and the fact that Radio 1 played the Undertones, the White Stripes and the Strokes today showed just how relevant he remained throughout his career.'

Bradley continued: 'No one thought that John Peel would ever die – he should have gone on and on. He was here in Derry in 2000 because he was presenting a documentary about the Undertones, and someone said something about the "respect" he was held in, and he was very uncomfortable with that. He enjoyed what he did, but he never put much of a real value on it. He was very quick to say, "All I do is play records." He never tried to be a star, and that's maybe why he never lost his focus.'

Manic Street Preachers singer-guitarist James Dean Bradfield was also one of the first to send his condolences. '[Peel] was a lifeline to hearing music I would never have heard otherwise,' he said. 'The service he provided was getting to hear music that you couldn't buy in Cardiff. He was a portal to a whole new world.' Former Led Zeppelin singer Robert Plant agreed: 'From my earliest recollections, John Peel championed and gave life to such a vivid and dynamic variety of music. His uniqueness was reflected in his continued popularity over four decades. He gave us airplay in the early days, when we were considered taboo by the BBC identikit disc jockey.'

Bernard Sumner, formerly of both Joy Division and New Order, said: 'This is a dreadful shock. He was one of the few people to give bands that played alternative music a chance to be heard, and he continued to be a champion of cutting-edge music throughout his life. He will be genuinely missed by millions of music fans all over the world, both inside and outside the music industry. Our thoughts are with his family.' While Billy Bragg said Peel had 'defined independent music,' adding: 'Although he became an institution at the BBC, he was, in effect, running his own pirate radio station from within the corporation.' Kurt Wagner, of American alternative country rockers Lambchop, claimed that the DJ's influence had also long been felt far outside his home country. 'He was amazing. The records of the Peel sessions were available over here. And his radio show was one of the few ones we heard of over here. He was legendary.'

Paul Hartnoll of Orbital recalled their final session on Peel just a few months before: 'The last thing we ever did as Orbital was a live broadcast on his show in July, which was such an honour. He stood right next to the equipment watching us when he didn't have to be in his control room. He was one of the first DJs to play us, certainly on Radio 1.' He added: 'When we were teenagers we'd stay up listening to his show and taping things from it. Peel introduced me to "Blue Monday" by New Order, that bass drum riff and using a drum machine in that fashion. Without hearing that, who knows ...?' He concluded: 'Young people can be so narrow-minded in their determination to be right, but Peel showed us not to be so closed-minded. He is irreplaceable, not least because Radio 1 wouldn't give someone like Peel a job now.'

Courtney Love said: 'I heard on the plane to San Francisco and I cried. He was magical. He was a wizard. He got people right at the right moment. We dedicated our show [that night] to him.' Carl Barat of the Libertines added: 'I once heard he didn't like the Libertines, but God bless him all the same. I got the impression he really cared, so it's a sore loss for music. I salute him.' While Tim Wheeler of Ash concluded: 'No more Festive Fifties, no more Peel sessions, no more records played at the wrong speed ... He seemed like he'd always been there. He was my favourite DJ by miles, and a really warm, lovely man.'

Like so many others, musician Andy Roberts, who first met John back in the late sixties and had remained in touch with him over the years, claimed that: 'John handed me my career on a plate. I must be one of about a hundred thousand people who can say that. I was in a poetry band called the Liverpool Scene and he volunteered to produce our first album because he liked what we were doing. We probably got our record deal on the strength of his involvement. Who else but John would have thrown their weight behind a poetry band?' Andy McCluskey, formerly of Orchestral Manoeuvres in the Dark, said it was a 'hugely sad day. There will be many musicians and bands out there today who feel a debt of gratitude to John Peel. I am certainly one of them.'

Meanwhile, Glastonbury Festival founder Michael Eavis immediately announced that one of the stages at the festival would in future be known as 'the John Peel Tent'. Previously known simply as 'the New Tent', it was, he concluded, the most fitting tent of the many that now annually populated Glastonbury, as it was, inevitably, the one tent John could always be found lurking in when not presenting his links for Radio 1 or BBC 2 – still tramping around in the old anorak and wellies on cold wet days. In an interview broadcast on the BBC's local Somerset Sound radio station the day after John's death, Eavis recalled how he first met John at the age of eighteen and that he had been something of a musical guru for him. John 'always knew which band was going to make the grade.'

And still yet more tributes continued to pour in from all those he had either helped directly or simply touched in his own personal way. Damon Albarn of Blur: 'John Peel's patronage was for me, like countless other musicians, one of the most significant things that happened to us in our careers. The world is going to be a poorer place with his sudden departure.' Even Noel Gallagher of Oasis, whose records Peel pointedly never played, paid tribute: 'John Peel was a rare breed amongst radio DJs. His contribution to introducing new music to music fans in this country has been phenomenal and he will be sadly missed.'

Elvis Costello: 'Peel was the contradiction of every bad thing you could say about radio. He had an open mind about music, whether he was bringing the listener the Incredible String Band or the Fall, Mike Hart or Echo and the Bunnymen, and countless bands that appeared only to be heard on his great shows.' He added that whenever they met, mainly their brief conversations would be centred on their mutual love of Liverpool FC. 'A great man, a fabulous curmudgeon, he was as rare as the music that he loved.'

Pulp singer Jarvis Cocker: 'Peel stuck up for the "sore thumbs" of the music scene. It would be absolutely impossible to write a history of the last forty years of the British music scene without mentioning John Peel's name. He was one of those few people about whom you could truly say that the world would have been a much different place without him.' While Radiohead singer Thom Yorke declared that Peel had been his 'inspiration' since the age of fourteen. 'Who am I going to listen to now?' he said. 'I'm thinking about you. Thanks, John Peel.'

Laura Cantrell, one of the most recent new acts championed by Peel and now receiving more mainstream recognition, described him simply as a man with 'an unabashed love for music.' She added, on hearing of his death: 'I really treasure that I got to know the man and his family, to hear his stories, and to be welcomed by him and Sheila to Peel Acres. To experience his sense of humour, the great joy that he took in his life, was inspiring.' While Grinderswitch founding member Dru Lombar posted the following message on the band's website: 'I want to take a minute and pay my respects to the late John Peel from the BBC in England. Mr Peel was a fan of Grinderswitch and for many years used "Pickin' the Blues" from the *Macon Tracks* album as his theme song. He was a strong influence on the British music scene and I know his fans will miss him.'

In terms of John's influence on the changes music went through in the late seventies, however, Geoff Barton, a lifelong mainstream rock fan, feels that 'too much emphasis is sometimes put now, I think, on what he did for punk and his career in the aftermath of that era. While there's no doubting he was the one responsible for first bringing the world Joy Division and the Smiths etc, it's important not to forget what a tremendous impact John had on music way before punk came along. For instance, I seem to recall him reciting a children's poem on an early Tyrannosaurus Rex album, one of those whimsical moments that could only have happened in the late sixties or very early seventies. Therefore I find it hard to reconcile the image I have of him with this godfather-of-punk label so many pundits stick him with now. The great thing about the Peel show was that it was always much more than the sum of its parts – and no matter how big, punk was only one part.'

Andy Kershaw naturally led the way with the tributes from fellow Radio 1 DJs and former presenters. Describing Peel as 'the single most important figure in the history of British rock music,' Kershaw went as far as to claim he would put the name John Peel 'ahead even of Paul McCartney and John Lennon, such was his vast contribution to the history of popular music over the last forty years.' He later added: 'If I were a sixteen-year-old kid tonight in a band, dreaming of making it big, I would be thinking my chances were far less than they were yesterday.' Peel was 'more important than any artist because he was the enthusiast who discovered so many of those whom we think of as the big figures of pop over the past forty years.' Jenny Abramsky, the BBC's controller of network radio, had been the one who broke the news to Kershaw, he later revealed. 'I've got some bad news for you,' she told him. 'I think you ought to sit down...'

Meanwhile, Andy's sister Liz Kershaw, a former Radio 1 DJ and now lunchtime presenter at the digital radio channel BBC 6 Music, said John was 'the least musically snooty person we know. He was utterly sincere in what he was doing, not because he wanted to be famous but because he thought he was on a mission to bring stuff to people's ears. He really did trawl through mailbags of demo cassettes. That's why we had Pulp and T. Rex, because he'd been discovering bands like that since 1967.'

Radio 1 DJ Jo Whiley, who presented coverage of the Glastonbury Festival with Peel, said that regardless of personal musical taste – she recalled John muttering disapprovingly whenever she got excited about someone like REM or Coldplay taking to the Glastonbury stage – 'John was simply one of my favourite men in the whole world – as a music fan and presenter he was simply an inspiration.' While current Radio 1 breakfast show DJ Chris Moyles also became 'emotional' on his first programme after the news was announced, talking about his 'pal' Peely. The notorious motormouth was unusually solemn as he opened his breakfast show. His voice faltered as he described Peel as 'like a grandfather', which seemed rather stretching the point somewhat. Then added: 'We're getting loads of texts in saying, "Why are you still going on about it? Get over it, he's only a bloke." But he's not just a bloke. You don't understand. You don't understand how important he was from the music side of things. Everybody loved him, he was a mate. He was like a father, a grandfather to everyone at Radio 1. It's like losing a member of the family. So for all those people who are moaning – go screw yourselves.'

Even Radio 1 DJs who had traditionally been perceived as being the antithesis of Peel came out with heartfelt personal tributes. Former Radio 1 DJ, now Radio 2 afternoon presenter, Steve Wright, said: 'He was a great influence on me and I'm glad I knew John Peel.' Mark Goodier, the former Radio 1 chart presenter, said he was 'absolutely stunned' at the news. 'It is just a terrible shock to see him go at such a young age. He is one of the people I listened to as a kid, who made me want to do the job I've done for the last twenty-five years. He was a special talent, one of the very few people allowed by Radio 1 to do whatever he wanted, because what they got back was a remarkably unique individual and a broadcaster famous the world over.' He added: 'He seems to have been in our lives for ever and we would like him to have been around a little longer. He has been a very regular contributor to the BBC World Service for many years, and this news will shock and sadden people the world over.'

While Bruno Brookes had this to say: 'John Peel was so untypical of what Radio 1 was known for across the decades. When other DJs were doing Roadshows he was there sitting in his chair, choosing his music, probably the most eclectic collection of music I've heard on any radio station. He was the authority. There was never the sense that John must move on, because who was going to replace him?'

Even Noel Edmonds was moved to comment: 'John

was a huge talent.' While Dave Lee Travis, the man who John once sneeringly pointed out 'brought darts and snooker to the radio', now working for BBC local radio, admitted: 'John was a great DJ. He would go out on a limb and champion bands that not everybody would get.' While Sir Jimmy Savile, who John once admitted he could barely bring himself to speak of, paid tribute to what he called Peel's honesty. He said: 'Unlike the rest of us, if he didn't like the record he gave it the thumbs-down, no matter how big the star.'

As former Radio 1 controller Trevor Dann wrote in the *Independent*: '[John] became a broadcasting icon because he had no artifice, no style, no shtick. What you got across the table at an Indian restaurant was what you got on the radio: passion, honesty and an understated facility for language. Younger broadcasters described as the new John Peel have come and gone for forty years, but the original was always the best.'

Charles Shaar Murray, writing in the *Guardian*, recalled how: 'When I was a teenager growing up in Lace Curtain Land during the 1960s, John Peel's Sunday afternoon show was my lifeline. So much of the music that has stayed with me first reached me through Peel's show.' He added: 'Though I rarely listened to his show in the past few years, it was a comfort to know that it, and he, were still there. I cannot imagine anyone else currently on UK music radio being able to match his

With Elton John at the 1977 Reading Festival. (*Rex Features*)

Football was probably the only religion for John Peel.
(*Neil Matthews/Rex Features*)

Presenting *Top of the Pops* with Kylie (*BBC*); and rather more relaxed on stage with old pal Jarvis Cocker (*BBC*), and with Ivor Cutler, one of the few remaining links between the long-haired, flared-trousered Peel of *The Perfumed Garden* and the Peel of the punk era and beyond. (*Retna*)

Covering Glastonbury for the BBC, Peel famously gave the main stage a wide berth, and found greater inspiration from the likes of the world stage, the dance tent and Glastonbury Tor. (*clockwise from left: Dave Young, PA, BBC*)

Indisputably the greatest record collection on the planet, said, according to the *NME*, to contain 26,000 vinyl LPs, 40,000 7" singles, and 40,000 CDs. (*Scope*)

The balding slightly overweight taxi-driver (as Peel frequently described himself) broadcasts to the nation (*Eva Vermandel/Katz Pictures*); and brings his downbeat, home-spun charm to an insurance ad. (*Retna*)

With Sheila (above) and relaxing (below) at Peel Acres.
(*Eleanor Bentall/Katz Pictures; Retna*)

(*Overleaf: Hugo Glendinning, Katz Pictures*)

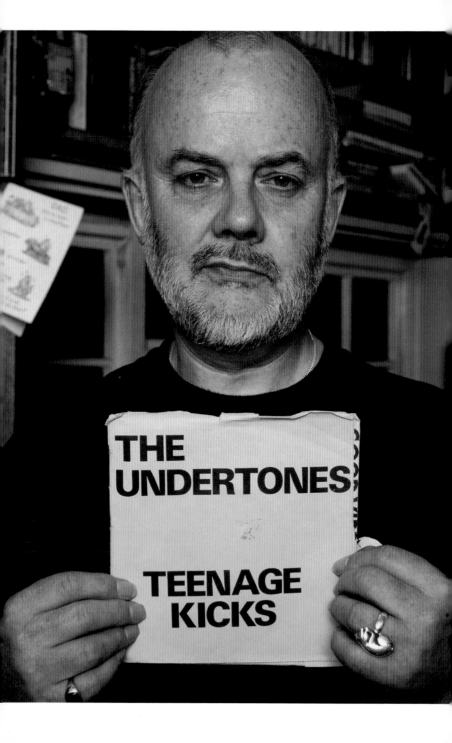

unique combination of taste and dedication. John Peel will prove irreplaceable.'

Adding to his initial press statement, current BBC Radio 1 controller Andy Parfitt told journalists: 'John's influence has towered over the development of popular music for nearly four decades and his contribution to modern music and music culture is immeasurable.' He added that John's death had 'absolutely devastated everyone. It is absolutely shocking news. We're stunned and bereft. He's irreplaceable because what he had was thirty-seven years of commitment to young music. Young music-makers respected him, and you can't get that without doing it and living it for thirty-seven years, and John did that.

'At Radio 1 gatherings,' Parfitt recalled, 'the DJs would gather around his chair like a throne while he told all these fantastic stories. He had a completely adventurous ear, he was totally engaged by new things that were happening. Hopeful bands all over the world sent their demo tapes to John knowing that he really cared. His commitment and passion for new music only grew stronger over the years ... Sometimes he disappeared into the tributaries of music, but all the time pushing forward and pushing forward. With John, age wasn't the issue: he was just totally committed and passionate about music and everyone respected him for that.'

Former Radio 1 DJ Charlie Gillett could only concur:

'John was the epitome of the DJ who plays only what he wants to play. He was in America in the 1960s when a whole lot of maverick people were let loose on FM radio to play what they liked, and I think he got infected with that idea ... I don't think everything he played was great and I don't know if he did either. But I don't think that was the point for him. Those of us who want to do what he did only do so because we're convinced we like the right things – I'm very snobby that way. But he wasn't like that at all.'

Bryan Gallagher, who wrote and presented a regular weekly column on *Home Truths* – and who John once memorably described as 'the jewel in the *Home Truths* crown' (for weeks afterwards his family said things like 'Tell the jewel his tea is ready') – did a special piece for Radio 4 that week in which he described the simple warmth of the man. 'I only met him once face to face but John spoke to me as if he had known me all my life,' Gallagher said. He added: 'John loathed the word "celebrity" – his great gift was his wonderful modesty. He could "walk with kings nor lose the common touch".' Gallagher had been busy writing his latest column for that week's show when he heard the news. 'I was actually just sitting there wondering if John would like it,' he recalled, when the announcement came on the radio. (Gallagher is now publishing a book of his collected *Home Truths* stories.)

And of course there were also hundreds of emails and

letters sent to newspapers. One such letter, from Greg McDonald of the Dawn Parade (a little-known indie band from East Anglia which John had loyally supported) and published in *The Times* on 28 October, expressed the feelings of many when it said: 'John Peel was that rarest of things: someone who really cared. Nobody has given more to British music. To the likes of us – a struggling indie band from East Anglia – Peel meant everything. He played every record we released. In the past few years I've spent on tour, the indie music world has radiated negativity about everyone – colleagues, recording companies, the media – but you never heard a bad word from anyone in a band about John Peel.'

Another letter published in *The Times* that day, from Juliet Shield in Liverpool, recalled an incident that showed the measure of the man and his deep-felt relationship with his listeners. She wrote: 'John Peel was a great lifter of spirits, and not only in the music world. One night in the early eighties he was having dinner in my restaurant in Liverpool with the late poet Adrian Henri. As I sat with them afterwards, I told John that our newly arrived German au pair was finding it very difficult to settle in, and that she was a big fan of his. "Tell her to listen in to Radio 1 at around eight on Monday evening," he said. Sure enough, right on schedule, he said: "This is for Eva, staying in Liverpool just now. You are a very lucky girl to be in a great city with the best football team in the world." It changed her whole outlook.'

Even the Prime Minister took time out to issue a statement. Tony Blair stopped just short of actually calling John 'the People's DJ', though it would not have been an unjust summary. But Mr Blair's official spokesman did make a point of telling reporters how 'genuinely saddened' the PM was by the news. 'His view is, John Peel was a genuine one-off, whether on Radio 1 or Radio 4. He was a unique voice in British broadcasting and used that voice to unearth new talent and different subjects and make them accessible to a much wider audience,' he said. While the *Sun* – which John detested long before their disgraceful coverage of the Hillsborough tragedy that made the paper permanently unpopular on Merseyside – ran a wonderfully funny but genuinely touching cartoon on their leader page the day after his death was announced. In it, an aged, white-bearded St Peter is depicted welcoming John and his large box of records to heaven. 'John Peel!' St Peter exclaims. 'I was listening to you when I was a lad...'

There had been a range of different guest presenters looking after his thrice-weekly slot on Radio 1 while John was away. But the Peel programme broadcast the same day the news of his death was announced was given over to a nicely put-together special 'tribute' show hosted by Steve Lamacq, one of the current

generation of radio presenters clearly influenced by
Peel. The entire show, as would all three Peel shows that
week, featured back-to-back selections from all the
many sessions and groundbreaking records John had
championed over the years, as well as broadcasting
some of the thousands of heartfelt messages the Radio 1
website had received via email. It featured a suitably
eclectic mix of Peel favourites like the Fall, the Smiths,
the Faces, Culture and something from the last Orbital
session. 'John had about ten all-time favourite sessions,'
Lamacq joked, at one point. At another, rather
poignantly, he invited listeners to fill a glass with red
wine and join him in a toast to Peely ...

Radio 4 also dropped their planned edition of *Home
Truths* the following Saturday. Instead, the writer and
poet Roger McGough, a long-time Peel pal and fellow
Liverpudlian, presented a special 'tribute' edition of the
show, featuring snippets from some of the funniest and
most deeply poignant moments from the six years John
was at its helm. On BBC 2 nearly two weeks later, Jo
Whiley introduced a special programme, consisting of
half an hour of tributes, followed by a repeat showing
of the hour-long documentary made to mark his sixtieth
birthday.

But perhaps the most heartfelt appreciation came
via Kershaw, who turned his Sunday night Radio 3
programme that week over to a show specially
dedicated to his former friend and mentor. Beginning

with Grinderswitch's 'Pickin' the Blues', he segued into 'One Man Guy', the slow country ballad by Loudon Wainwright that could have been written about Peel himself. 'This is one programme I never wanted to have to present,' Kershaw said by way of introduction. But rather than being unduly morose – 'something John would have hated' – the show would, instead, be a 'celebration of John's life.' He added that John had been contemptuous of the trend at football grounds recently to indulge in minute-silences at every opportunity, whether the recipient had anything to do with football or not. 'So instead of a minute's silence,' he announced, 'we present an hour and fifteen minutes of noise!', before going straight into 'New Rose' by the Damned, followed by a track from an early Jimi Hendrix session recorded for *Top Gear* in 1967 – the guitarist's wonderfully warped version of Bob Dylan's 'Can You Please Crawl Out Your Window?'.

When Kershaw later played the Bhundu Boys' 'Hupenyu Hwangu' (translation: 'My Happy Life as a Musician') from *Shabini*, an album John loved, he recalled the two of them going to see the Bhundu Boys play at a college in Chelsea. 'Halfway through I turned round to see the tears streaming down John's face. He said he thought it was the most natural flowing music he'd ever heard in his life.'

One thing Andy didn't mention on the programme, however, was the huge row behind the scenes at the

BBC caused by a story he had written for the *Independent*, published earlier that week. In it, Kershaw explained how, at the time of his death, the Peel show – the longest-running, most consistently popular programme in the history of Radio 1 – had recently been shunted back an hour from its established ten till midnight slot, to eleven till one, and that the last time he had seen him John 'looked absolutely worn out. We went to a café near Radio 1 and I said "John, you look terrible."' He claimed John replied that the combination of his new, later Radio 1 slot and presenting *Home Truths* 'is killing me.' Kershaw added: 'He felt he had been marginalized.' He repeated the claims later that same day on a Channel Four News broadcast, and they were instantly picked up and reported across all the major news outlets the next day.

The BBC hit back at Kershaw's claims, issuing a press statement in which they insisted the move to a later time slot for the show had been made 'to give a wider audience to new specialist music shows'. They pointed out that Peel had agreed to the changes after a meeting with Andy Parfitt, the controller of Radio 1.

However, *The Times* reported that Parfitt was so concerned at the allegations made by Kershaw that Peel's studio producers had been asked if he had made any off-the-record complaints to them. They said that he had not. As a result, BBC executives were said to be 'furious' with Kershaw. One said: 'It is extremely distressing that Andy should say this. John was fully supportive of the changes – he even said that the late finish meant clearer roads when he drove back to East Anglia.'

The BBC also claimed that John had rejected the idea of prerecording his Radio 1 shows, which were by then alternating between two programmes a week live from London, with the Thursday programme broadcast from his home studio. There was also an official statement from Radio 1, which read: 'Everyone at the BBC is shocked and upset by John's sudden death. At a time when his family are still in deep mourning – out of respect for them – this is not the time to make remarks or to comment.'

Inevitably, perhaps, there was at least one article in the newspapers that refused to get damp-eyed about Peel's passing. Almost as inevitably it came from Tony Parsons, who wrote in the *Daily Mirror* how 'overrated' he always felt the Peel show was, in a strangely sour reprise of what he and his now ex-wife Julie Burchill had written all those years ago in *The Boy Looked At Johnny*. No longer able to accuse his target of being 'too old', Parsons was reduced to claiming that Tony Blackburn had always been a better DJ than Peel; a strangely pointless assertion, snide and thoughtless – everything John was not, in fact.

When I spoke with *Mojo* editor-in-chief Phil Alexander on the day the Parsons article was published, he told me he was 'still in pain over it'. Comparing Parsons' early career as the self-styled *enfant terrible* of the *NME*, and now as the writer of lad-lit novels, with what Peel managed to achieve in his own career, he added: 'I think what really gets Parsons is that Peel was virtually impregnable to the views of people like him. At the end of the day, John never begged anyone to listen to his programme. Indeed, I'd speculate that it's doubtful someone like Parsons has even heard a Peel show in thirty years. But there you go, that's what he does for a living, I suppose, stirring the shit. Claiming Tony Blackburn was a much better Radio 1 DJ back in the seventies than John Peel – I mean, come on! It's just courting controversy for controversy's sake.'

By contrast, Alexander, who had actually known John, recalled how, 'Right up to his last few shows, John was still digging deeper than anyone else to try and bring us the music we would simply never have heard otherwise. In more recent times, I remember him best as the guy who championed extreme dance artists like Richie Hawtin – previously known as Plastic Man. In recent months, I also noticed that John was getting into the UK "grind" scene, a sort of post-dance, post-drum'n'bass, electronic hodgepodge that particularly appealed to him. As a result, he was the first to play John E Cash and all those kind of people.

'I remember taking part with John in one of those big

One Live events that Radio 1 do sometimes where they take over an entire town for a week. This was in Birmingham a couple of years ago, and I remember arriving with Mary Anne Hobbs at this club somewhere in town, ready to take over broadcasting from John at midnight. Richie Hawtin was on stage at the time, doing this absolutely mental set, like being hit with an anvil to the side of the head at incredible speed! It was so inescapably loud I literally couldn't hear myself think – and I've been to plenty of noisy gigs. Then I saw John standing there with a glass of red wine in his hand, head going, totally and utterly into it. I thought, God, how does he do it? I'm half his age and I've been to a few "loud" gigs in my time, but even I'm having trouble handling this …

'The thing that most people probably don't realise, though, was how much preparation he put into his shows. On air he always liked to affect the sort of lazy, laconic style that gave you the impression he was almost making up the running order as he went along. But I know from having seen him work just how meticulous he was, and how far ahead he always planned. Everybody knows he had this great, obsessive love of music, but it was his organisation of that obsession that helped make his shows so great. Despite the impression he gave, he didn't wade in in a disorganised manner, John was always a very serious, very attentive listener who would literally spend eight hours a day going through the hundreds of records and CDs he was sent every week.'

As proof, Phil pointed to the special editions of the Peel show that Radio 1 were going to be broadcasting that week (the second week after his death). 'All the shows will be featuring music John had already picked before he went away on holiday with Sheila. He never liked leaving anything to the last minute. A quite good show was never good enough for a Peel programme; they all had to be great in their own right. And unlike most radio presenters, nothing on John's shows was looked after by other people. He had a small two-person production team – producer Louise and broadcast assistant Dave, both young enough to be his own kids – who were always very good. But all the key decisions in the latter years would be made by John. Which is another reason why his shows and style of presentation lasted so well over the years, I think. No matter who "produced" them or what music he chose to play, they were all indelibly stamped with Peel's personality and vision, his understated authority.

'People used to say that once an artist he had championed started to make it in the mainstream, he immediately abandoned them and stopped playing their records. But that wasn't strictly true, nor was it a fair reflection on the reasons why he would usually move on. It wasn't the fact of success that turned John off. He was pretty darn successful himself, let's not forget. It was more whether the music would stand the test of that transition and if the artists would still continue to produce stuff that was as enthralling as their earlier efforts. Almost always, in his view, the answer was in the negative. But there were several notable exceptions, like PJ Harvey and Orbital, both of whom had recorded sessions for the show over the course of the last year.

'A lot of the obscuria John would unearth didn't amount to much at times, but it was his endless quest for it that endured and made such compelling listening. And it really did go on right till the very end. For example, I think the very last live session he broadcast on his show before leaving for Peru was by an American singer called Phillip Roebuck – a sort of one-man-band who records alone and puts out records on his own obscure little label. Other than that, no one knows who he is. He was just another guy John had brought into the studio to record a session, now likely to remain an enigma.'

Phil also pointed to the final phone call John had made to his office in London, requesting they search out indie labels in Peru. Hosting the second of the three special tribute shows aired on Radio 1 in Peel's slot the week he died, Mary Anne Hobbs had broadcast a snippet from the message John left on the office answer-machine. Phil said hearing it really brought home to him just how dedicated John was.

'That's the thing about Peel. For him, it was always more than just a job; it was always entirely personal, really. Unlike most of us who really do want to get away from it all while we're on holiday, part of the fun for John was checking out the local record shops, the local music scene. Even though he knew he'd never be able to listen to all the records he already had, he was still searching for something new, something more, right till the end. He was a genuine, irrepressible, life-long fan. It's a cliché but for once it's actually true: there really won't be anyone else like him again.'

Although John calculated that only 'about five per cent' of the hundreds of thousands of recordings he owned were actually 'crucial to my life', within days of his death, behind the scenes a 'bidding war' was reported to have broken out for his vast and unique record collection. With offers reputedly starting at £1 million, both the British Library and an anonymous US radio company were said to have already expressed 'serious interest' in acquiring what must be the most unique, not to mention vast, record collection in existence.

In his final years, John made no secret of the fact that he saw the collection, he told friends, as 'my pension'. The final tally at the time of his death was believed to have been in the region of 26,000 LPs, 40,000 CDs and 40,000 seven-inch singles. His manager and close friend Clive Selwood told the *Daily Record*: 'We had a phone call from an American radio company offering us over £1 million. It's a very important collection. John always felt that, when the time came, it would be a pension for his wife Sheila. He had also been talking to the British Library about buying the collection and they had mentioned a similar amount. It's priceless. It's got all his annotations on it. He even had to extend his house and reinforce the floor to hold it all.' The haul contains rare promos and signed discs from the Rolling Stones and the Beatles.

Within forty-eight hours of the announcement of John's death, unsubstantiated rumours were already flying that the Undertones would be re-releasing 'Teenage Kicks' in John's 'honour'. Bookies William Hill had even begun to give odds of 14/1 on 'Teenage Kicks' being the No. 1 single for Christmas, making it fourth favourite behind the planned Band Aid single. It was exactly the sort of cheap media circus John would have deplored. But William Hill spokesman Rupert Adams said: 'Over the last few days we have been repeatedly asked if we will be offering any prices on ["Teenage Kicks"] being a Christmas hit. It is a tribute to Peel's popularity that music fans are making so many enquiries.'

Thankfully, in a gesture that would no doubt have reduced Peel to more of his familiar tears, the Undertones made an official announcement the next day flatly denying they would be re-releasing 'Teenage

Kicks'. As the band's manager Andy Ferguson said: 'It would be totally inappropriate to release "Teenage Kicks" as a single and is not something the band would even consider.'

John's last ever interview, conducted at home in his sitting room, just six weeks before he died, was with a young reporter named Sophie Wilcockson from the Liverpool University alumni magazine *Insight*. She recalled, in an article in the *Daily Telegraph*, how he gave her more than three hours of his time that day – a typically generous gesture from a man whose core constituency throughout his long career had always been students.

Wilcockson later recalled how he had talked a great deal about Sheila and his great love for her, and how much they were both looking forward to his forthcoming trip to Peru, despite his fear of flying. When asked what his biggest fear was, though, he replied: 'Death, I guess. The fact of it and the manner of it, really.'

Asked which records from his vast collection he'd replace first in the event of a fire, he pointed out that the problem was that many were, quite literally, irreplaceable. And while it was well-known, of course, that in recent years John had maintained that when he died, apart from playing 'Teenage Kicks' at his funeral, which he fully expected, he also wanted the opening lyrics to the song – to wit: 'Teenage dreams, so hard to beat' – as his epitaph on his gravestone, he also revealed to Wilcockson some other hitherto-unknown selections he thought might be appropriate for such an occasion.

'Roger Milla' by Pépé Kallé – celebrating the famous Cameroonian footballer who'd made a great impression on the 1990 World Cup in Italy, at the official age of thirty-eight (though some reckoned he was already into his forties) – was currently the song he most enjoyed imagining being played at his funeral, he said, because, like 'Teenage Kicks', it was 'such an uplifting, glorious record. I would need to have something like that at my funeral. Then I would probably settle for a Fall compilation of some sort, I think.'

Death was not yet something he was willing to countenance for too long, however. He told Wilcockson he could easily envisage himself as a DJ at seventy or even eighty years of age. 'I'm still looking for the next Elvis,' he insisted, as always. 'The next thing that will seem so astonishing to me that it's almost frightening.'

More generally, away from music and back in the grisly real world, he said he felt let down by New Labour. After Blair's 'kowtowing' to Bush, he couldn't, he said, 'in all conscience vote Labour now.' He had campaigned, briefly, for John Prescott but he was 'a shy man' and 'not tremendously good at that sort of thing'. He had even been on the campaign bus, at one point, but had just 'sat there, nervously looking out of the window. So I wasn't much use.'

The day his death was announced in the newspapers, John's picture made the front page of *The Times*, the *Guardian*, the *Daily Telegraph*, the *Independent*, the *Daily Mail*, the *Daily Express* and even the *Sun*, while in the weeks that followed his face graced the covers of the *NME*, *Word* and *Mojo*, while BBC 2, VH1, MTV and the Biography Channel all broadcast tribute programmes. Above and beyond the sea of heartfelt tributes, however, lies a phenomenon not entirely explained by the man's obvious charm and talent, or even his irresistibly amusing way with words.

The only other modern-day radio presenter I can think of who received a similarly rich vein of loyalty and respect from his audience was, perhaps, the former *Today* presenter on Radio 4, the determinedly no-nonsense Brian Redhead, who died in 1993. Though known for two very different types of programme, in their own highly individual ways, both men could be said to have personified the delectable intimacy of radio broadcasting at its most serious, most meaningful level. That's why, just like me, who shared only a few words with him on those all too rare but always memorable occasions our paths crossed, there are millions of people out there who sincerely believe that we knew John Peel. Like Redhead, he really was a friend. Not one that would pop in for a cup of tea, but one that would always be there, no matter what, ready to regale us with another example of his rare and inscrutable magic.

John was simply one of those people who genuinely believed that radio had just as much to offer in its own way as television, possibly even more. Unlike TV, radio streams into the homes, cars, schools and workplaces of the nation with a universality uncommon to any other media. It stays effortlessly with us, whether we are listening closely or busy doing other things, a constant presence with an unparalleled capacity, at its best, to entertain, stimulate and inform. John Peel knew this as instinctively as if it were part of his DNA code.

At their best, both his Radio 1 shows – the memory and history of which will stand as a monument to public service broadcasting for eternity – and his equally applauded if, sadly, shorter-lived *Home Truths* programme had one thing in common, whatever your age or musical likes and dislikes: they left you wondering at the infinite variations of human existence, the marvellous things we all seem to have in common, plus some of the things that clearly we do not. Or as Brian Eno said on the radio the week John died: 'There was a real consistency in the John Peel [Radio 1] show and *Home Truths*. He was a democrat, looking for beauty and interest in both the lives and music of ordinary folk.'

His favourite trick, of course, was to play back to back records that appeared, on first hearing, so appallingly incongruous it actually stopped you in your tracks and made you listen, constantly questioning your assumptions about what you were hearing and what you had just been listening to before, all so different, yet all so important somehow. Peel was the first DJ to perfect the art of playing you something you didn't know you liked – until Peel played it to you.

His funeral was held on Friday, 12 November 2004. The service was held at St Edmundsbury Cathedral, in Bury St Edmunds, not far from the lay-by where John had presented Sheila with her new Morgan eight years before. True to the great public serviceman's spirit, it was announced that the funeral would be open to the public, and on the day barriers had to be erected to clear the way for the cortège as several thousand people came to pay their last respects in person.

The service was broadcast to the crowd via specially mounted speakers. According to former Radio 1 DJ Johnnie Walker, who had known John since their days on the pirates (Walker broadcast for Radio Caroline), speaking by phone later that afternoon to Radio 2, the presence of so many members of the public 'really added to the occasion,' describing how the crowd outside had burst into spontaneous applause as the coffin was carried from the cathedral to the tune of 'Teenage Kicks'.

Apart from friends and family, there were famous faces like Jarvis Cocker, Jack White, Billy Bragg, Joan Armatrading, Feargal Sharkey, Robert Plant ... Sir Elton John sent a floral tribute which was placed by the doors of the cathedral, along with a simple handwritten note, which read: 'Thank you for all the Great Music. You were a hero for so many, much love, Elton.' Also present were Andy Kershaw, Jo Whiley, David Jensen, Bob Harris, Annie Nightingale, Delia Smith, Griff Rhys Jones, amongst many other friends and colleagues from John's long career.

The funeral was conducted by Canon Deirdre Parmenter, Rural Dean of Stowmarket, who had first met Peel and his family when they participated in local events. During the service traditional church songs, including 'Abide With Me', were sung by the Stowmarket Choral Society, of which Sheila is a member. Then later, during the eulogies, the assembled throng were regaled by Roy Orbison's 'Running Scared' and Howlin Wolf's 'Going Down Slow', the latter including the line: 'If I never get well no more, I have had my fun ...'

Paul Gambaccini led the way with a long and heartfelt eulogy, in which he described John as 'the most-heard and most-loved broadcaster of all time' who had 'meant something to successive generations.' He added that he had always expected it would be John Walters who delivered the eulogy at Peel's funeral. 'But he got out of that job a couple of years ago.'

John's brother Alan, who looks uncannily like John, pointed to his brother's devotion to Sheila. 'He always said she was a stupendous wife and he was happy and proud to have ensnared her. He couldn't believe his luck,' he said.

John's children asked a friend to deliver a short speech – they feared they would break down if they tried to deliver it themselves, it was explained – on behalf of all four of them and their mother, Sheila. In it they thanked everybody who had sent cards, letters and flowers. 'Knowing that he meant so much to so many of you has made us all very proud,' they said in their written address. Among the many charming memories they shared was the illuminating admission that he was so hopeless with money that, 'Mum gave him pocket money for twenty-six years and he finally got access to a bank account at the age of fifty-five.'

They added that they had been asked all their lives what it was like to have John Peel as a father. Their reply was this: 'He was a lot cooler, more culturally aware and popular than we were. We have never had another dad and couldn't have wished for a better one.'

At the end of the funeral, as guests prepared to head off to a private reception, John's voice burst out of the speakers, accompanied by the distinctive 'Let's Go Tripping!' by Dick Dale, now better known to Radio 4 listeners as the signature tune to *Home Truths*. Part of a montage producers of the programme had broadcast on the tribute edition of the show a couple of weeks before, John could be heard describing his life. 'I'm fabulously lucky,' he was heard saying. 'I've got everything I ever wanted as a kid – a house in the country with dogs and cats, an astounding wife, really nice children, and a job I like, playing records on the radio. It's difficult to think what could be added to this.' In another excerpt, John added: 'If I drop dead tomorrow, I couldn't really complain. I hope I don't, because there's going to be a Fall album next year and I'd like to hear it.' Then his voice faded, to be replaced by the sound of the Kop singing 'You'll Never Walk Alone'.

Sheila wept quietly as she and the children followed the coffin slowly out of the church to the sound of long applause from the crowd. As Johnnie Walker commented later that day: 'It was a magnificent send-off, really beautiful.'

As to what kind of memorial John Peel should have, there had already been many suggestions made before the funeral had even taken place, such was the fervour to put forward some form of official commemoration. The BBC said they would be consulting with John's family on plans for a fitting memorial in due course. And, as befitting the more discerning audience Peel always attracted, there were no requests posted for any 'special fountains'. Instead, a poster on the Fall's official website suggested that, rather than a minute's silence, there should be a minute of noise, as that would be 'what Peel would have wanted'. Others suggested some form of statue, perhaps placed somewhere at his beloved Anfield, preferably with a view of the pitch from the part of the ground known in his youth as the Kop. At the very least, some suggested, there should be some form of plaque placed at the BBC.

The suggestion that briefly captured my imagination was the rather poignant one that all the new bands Peel had ever played for the first time on his show should go up to Broadcasting House in London and lay a copy of their debut single on the steps, in the manner of a ceremonial floral tribute. The bitter irony is that there is now no one left at BBC radio who would even consider playing most of them. One still-grieving critic suggested that a more 'fittingly morose sight' would be to place the records in a line stretching all the way forlornly down Regent Street ...

The sad fact is, for any of the distraught fans out there wondering who the 'next John Peel' will be, there is frankly no one at Radio 1, nor any other station in the world, who could possibly guarantee the vastly eclectic musical universe Peel routinely created for us for nearly forty years. As a Radio 1 spokesman said when asked who would be replacing Peel in the eleven to one slot from now on: 'John is irreplaceable.' He added: 'Radio 1's commitment to new music will be reflected in late-night programmes which are a fitting tribute to him.' Of course it would. But from now on it would have to do it without John Peel. That made its night-time output another thing entirely, fitting or not.

The Peel autobiography had been due for delivery to Transworld, the publishers, in March 2005, ready for publication the following autumn. What will happen to the book now is not known for sure as I write these final words. The decision, ultimately, will be Sheila's, though much will depend, of course, on how much of the book John had actually completed by the time he died.

In one recent interview John was quoted as saying he had written as much as 45,000 words – about half the manuscript, though he complained he had only got as far as his first trip to America. However, in other interviews he claimed to have written less than 15,000 words, mainly covering his troubled childhood. Until more is known, the official word from Transworld, a division of the giant Random House conglomerate, is that it is 'too early to know' whether the book will now go ahead. Transworld managing director Larry Finlay said: 'It's a very, very sad day. It's tragic and we are all very shocked. It's just too early to know what will happen. John said in his radio broadcasts that he was regularly getting on with the writing, but a lot now will depend on what Sheila – to whom we send our deepest sympathies – wants.'

It seems unfair that someone with such a wonderfully warm and generous heart should die of a heart attack. Maybe he had just given so much of it away. Which is why, finally, like Elvis and the Undertones, John Peel will remain as ageless, classless and palpably with us as ever. The greatest cultural arbiter music radio has ever known.

As John's old editor at *Sounds*, Alan Lewis, says: 'John's show became almost critic-proof, to a degree, in a way that simply wouldn't be possible today for a new young DJ on Radio 1. With the onset of the internet and multi-channel TV and radio, Radio 1 doesn't have anything like the same reach and dominance now that it had back in the sixties and seventies. And that gave John incredible power. He didn't abuse it but he did have power, and deep down inside he knew that. He had influence because he was a maverick but also because for most of his career at the BBC there was simply nowhere else for the audience to go. No commercial radio until the late seventies, certainly no XFM or Kiss until the last decade. His success went hand-in-hand with the value of being a public service broadcaster.

'As such,' says Lewis, 'there can literally be no replacement. Radio 1 has many well-known personalities fronting their shows these days, all quite radical in their own way – from Tim Westwood to Steve Lamacq. But none of their various specialist shows – from rock to rap to dance and techno – would have to end if the DJ suddenly left. With Peel that's not the case. He literally *was* the programme. You can't just bring someone in, no matter how talented or well-meaning, and say this is the John Peel show but with a new presenter. John's show, his style of presentation, his musical taste and personal style, all went with him when he died.'

Of all the many warm and wonderful memories and anecdotes that poured forth in the days after his death, the one that, for me, sums up the size of the loss we have all incurred in his passing, whether we ever heard or enjoyed one of his shows or not, is the one his old friend and fellow Radio 1 survivor Annie Nightingale told. Nightingale recalled how the week before he and Sheila set off for Peru, she and John had both attended a special dinner at a Notting Hill restaurant organised by the bigwigs at Radio 1 to honour all its specialist DJs.

'He was,' she said, 'as always amongst his peer group, the centre of attention and originator of many of the laughs we had. His latest discovery, he said, was a band called Steveless. "They make an LP [John never said album] every week. They're called Steveless because there's no one in the band called Steve." I don't know what Steveless or I, or anyone else who loves music, is going to do without John.'

Festive 50s

The shifting nature of John Peel's Radio 1 audience is evident through the twenty-seven years of the Festive 50 – particularly if one compares the listeners' poll of all-time fifty tracks voted for in 1976 with the same chart in, say, 1981. From 1982 onwards the Festive 50 became a poll of the listeners' favourite 50 tracks from the year in question. Such was the paucity of entries in 1997, Peel opted for a Festive 31. In 1977 family problems, notably the difficult birth of his first daughter Alexandra, meant that Peel just listed a few of his favourite tracks from the year.

1976

1	Led Zeppelin	Stairway To Heaven
2	Derek & the Dominoes	Layla
3	Bob Dylan	Desolation Row
4	Pink Floyd	Echoes
5	Jimi Hendrix	All Along the Watchtower
6	Free	All Right Now
7	Racing Cars	They Shoot Horses, Don't They?
8	Pink Floyd	Shine On You Crazy Diamond
9	The Beatles	A Day in the Life
10	Bob Dylan	Like A Rolling Stone
11	Poco	Rose of Cimarron
12	Neil Young	Cortez the Killer
13	The Rolling Stones	Brown Sugar
14	The Beatles	Hey Jude
15	Legendary Stardust Cowboy	Paralysed

16	Jimi Hendrix	Voodoo Chile
17	The Beatles	Strawberry Fields Forever
18	Captain Beefheart	Big Eyed Beans From Venus
19	Led Zeppelin	Whole Lotta Love
20	Lynyrd Skynyrd	Freebird
21	Van Morrison	Madame George
22	The Doors	Riders on the Storm
23	Bob Dylan	Visions of Johanna
24	Jefferson Airplane	White Rabbit
25	Deep Purple	Child in Time
26	Little Feat	Long Distance Love
27	Grinderswitch	Pickin' the Blues
28	Joe Walsh	Rocky Mountain Way
29	The Who	Won't Get Fooled Again
30	The Misunderstood	I Can Take You to the Sun
31	Genesis	Supper's Ready
32	Bob Marley & the Wailers	No Woman, No Cry
33	Jonathan Richman	Roadrunner
34	Rod Stewart	Maggie May
35	Jackson Browne	Late For The Sky
36	Led Zeppelin	Kashmir
37	Jimi Hendrix	Hey Joe
38	The Allman Brothers Band	Jessica
39	The Rolling Stones	Jumping Jack Flash
40	Grateful Dead	Dark Star
41	Richard Thompson	I Wanna See the Bright Lights
42	Family	The Weaver's Answer
43	Jackson Browne	Fountain of Sorrow
44	Bob Dylan	Hurricane
45	The Doors	Light My Fire
46	Matching Mole	O Caroline
47	Roy Harper	When an Old Cricketer Leaves the Crease
48	Wild Man Fischer	Go To Rhino Records
49	Little Feat	Willin'
50	Yes	And You & I

1977

1	The Motors	Dancing the Night Away
2	Althea & Donna	Uptown Top Ranking
3	The Motors	You Beat the Hell Out of Me
4	The Rezillos	I Can't Stand My Baby
5	John Cooper Clarke	Suspended Sentence
6	The Desperate Bicycles	Smokescreen
7	Marlene Webber	Right Track
8	Neil Young	Like A Hurricane
9	The Clash	Complete Control
10	Frankie Miller	Be Good to Yourself
11	Sex Pistols	Holidays in the Sun
12	The Lurkers	Shadow
13	Jah Hayes/Ranking Trevor	Truly

1978

1	Sex Pistols	Anarchy in the UK
2	The Clash	Complete Control
3	Sex Pistols	God Save the Queen
4	Stiff Little Fingers	Suspect Device
5	Magazine	Shot By Both Sides
6	Sex Pistols	Pretty Vacant
7	The Clash	White Man in Hammersmith Palais
8	The Buzzcocks	What Do I Get?
9	Public Image Ltd.	Public Image
10	The Undertones	Teenage Kicks
11	Stiff Little Fingers	Alternative Ulster
12	The Buzzcocks	Boredom
13	The Damned	New Rose
14	Led Zeppelin	Stairway To Heaven
15	The Clash	White Riot
16	David Bowie	Heroes
17	The Only Ones	Another Girl, Another Planet

18	Sex Pistols	Holidays in the Sun
19	Lynyrd Skynyrd	Freebird
20	The Rezillos	I Can't Stand My Baby
21	Van Morrison	Madame George
22	Siouxsie & the Banshees	Hong Kong Garden
23	The Clash	Police & Thieves
24	The Jam	Down in the Tube Station at Midnight
25	Elvis Costello	Watching the Detectives
26	Bruce Springsteen	Born To Run
27	Ian Dury & the Blockheads	Sex & Drugs & Rock & Roll
28	Dire Straits	Sultans of Swing
29	Pink Floyd	Shine On You Crazy Diamond
30	The Buzzcocks	Moving Away From the Pulsebeat
31	Derek & the Dominoes	Layla
32	The Stranglers	Hanging Around
33	The Stranglers	No More Heroes
34	Siouxsie & the Banshees	Helter Skelter
35	The Motors	Dancing the Night Away
36	Bob Dylan	Like A Rolling Stone
37	Elvis Costello	Alison
38	Siouxsie & the Banshees	Overground
39	The Who	My Generation
40	The Stranglers	London Lady
41	Siouxsie & the Banshees	Switch
42	Siouxsie & the Banshees	Mirage
43	Siouxsie & the Banshees	Jigsaw Feeling
44	The Jam	In the City
45	Sex Pistols	EMI
46	Bob Dylan	Desolation Row
47	The Flying Lizards	Summertime Blues
48	Neil Young	Like A Hurricane
49	Thin Lizzy	Emerald
50	Siouxsie & the Banshees	Metal Postcard

1979

1	Sex Pistols	Anarchy in the UK
2	The Undertones	Teenage Kicks
3	The Clash	White Man in Hammersmith Palais
4	The Jam	Down in the Tube Station at Midnight
5	The Clash	Complete Control
6	Stiff Little Fingers	Alternative Ulster
7	Special AKA	Gangsters
8	Stiff Little Fingers	Suspect Device
9	Public Image Ltd.	Public Image
10	The Damned	New Rose
11	The Ruts	In A Rut
12	The Undertones	Get Over You
13	Sex Pistols	God Save the Queen
14	Sex Pistols	Holidays in the Sun
15	Stiff Little Fingers	Johnny Was
16	Sex Pistols	Pretty Vacant
17	Magazine	Shot By Both Sides
18	Stiff Little Fingers	Wasted Life
19	The Jam	Eton Rifles
20	The Only Ones	Another Girl, Another Planet
21	Siouxsie & the Banshees	Love in a Void
22	The Damned	Love Song
23	Gang of Four	Damaged Goods
24	Led Zeppelin	Stairway To Heaven
25	The Buzzcocks	Boredom
26	The Clash	White Riot
27	The Jam	Strange Town
28	Public Image Ltd.	Death Disco
29	The Undertones	You've Got My Number
30	Pink Floyd	Shine On You Crazy Diamond
31	The Undertones	Jimmy Jimmy
32	The Who	My Generation
33	Dead Kennedys	California Uber Alles

34	David Bowie	Heroes
35	Siouxsie & the Banshees	Icon
36	The Specials	Too Much Too Young
37	The Skids	Into the Valley
38	Siouxsie & the Banshees	Switch
39	Tubeway Army	Are Friends Electric?
40	The Fall	Rowche Rumble
41	The Mekons	Where Were You?
42	Siouxsie & the Banshees	Jigsaw Feeling
43	The Cure	10:15 Saturday Night
44	Siouxsie & the Banshees	Playground Twist
45	The Stranglers	No More Heroes
46	Siouxsie & the Banshees	Helter Skelter
47	The Ruts	Babylon's Burning
48	Siouxsie & the Banshees	Hong Kong Garden
49	The Clash	Police & Thieves
50	The Buzzcocks	What Do I Get?

1980

1	Sex Pistols	Anarchy in the UK
2	Joy Division	Atmosphere
3	Joy Division	Love Will Tear Us Apart
4	The Jam	Down in the Tube Station at Midnight
5	The Clash	White Man in Hammersmith Palais
6	Dead Kennedys	Holiday In Cambodia
7	The Undertones	Teenage Kicks
8	The Damned	New Rose
9	Stiff Little Fingers	Alternative Ulster
10	Joy Division	Transmission
11	Public Image Ltd.	Public Image
12	Sex Pistols	Holidays in the Sun
13	The Jam	Going Underground
14	Joy Division	Decades

Festive 50s

15	The Clash	Complete Control
16	Stiff Little Fingers	Johnny Was
17	The Undertones	Get Over You
18	The Cure	A Forest
19	The Ruts	In A Rut
20	Joy Division	New Dawn Fades
21	The Fall	Totally Wired
22	Joy Division	She's Lost Control
23	Sex Pistols	Pretty Vacant
24	Stiff Little Fingers	Suspect Device
25	Sex Pistols	God Save the Queen
26	The Fall	How I Wrote 'Elastic Man'
27	Stiff Little Fingers	Wasted life
28	The Only Ones	Another Girl, Another Planet
29	The Damned	Love Song
30	Adam & The Ants	Kings of the Wild Frontier
31	Dead Kennedys	California Über Alles
32	The Specials	Gangsters
33	Public Image Ltd.	Poptones
34	Public Image Ltd.	Careering
35	Killing Joke	Requiem
36	Killing Joke	Psyche
37	Siouxsie & the Banshees	Jigsaw Feeling
38	The Fall	Fiery Jack
39	The Clash	Armagideon Time
40	Spizz Energi	Where's Captain Kirk?
41	Joy Division	Twenty-Four Hours
42	The Damned	Smash It Up
43	The Teardrop Explodes	Treason
44	Siouxsie & the Banshees	Switch
45	Siouxsie & the Banshees	Icon
46	The Clash	Bank Robber
47	Siouxsie & the Banshees	Hong Kong Garden
48	The Clash	White Riot
49	The Fall	Rowche Rumble
50	Gang of Four	Damaged Goods
51	Siouxsie & the Banshees	Love In A Void

52	Killing Joke	Wardance
53	Adam & the Ants	Dog Eat Dog
54	The Ruts	West One (Shine On Me)
55	The Who	My Generation
56	The Mo-dettes	White Mice
57	Stiff Little Fingers	Tin Soldiers
58	The Stranglers	No More Heroes
59	The Jam	Eton Rifles
60	Pink Floyd	Shine On You Crazy Diamond
61	Magazine	Shot By Both Sides
62	Public Image Ltd.	Death Disco
63	Led Zeppelin	Stairway To Heaven
64	Joy Division	Dead Souls
65	Wah! Heat	Better Scream

1981

1	Joy Division	Atmosphere
2	Sex Pistols	Anarchy in the UK
3	Joy Division	Love Will Tear Us Apart
4	New Order	Ceremony
5	Joy Division	New Dawn Fades
6	The Undertones	Teenage Kicks
7	Joy Division	Decades
8	The Cure	A Forest
9	Dead Kennedys	Holiday In Cambodia
10	The Clash	White Man in Hammersmith Palais
11	Joy Division	Dead Souls
12	The Damned	New Rose
13	The Jam	Down in the Tube Station at Midnight
14	Joy Division	Transmission
15	Altered Images	Dead Pop Stars
16	Stiff Little Fingers	Alternative Ulster
17	Sex Pistols	Holidays in the Sun

18	The Clash	Complete Control
19	The Birthday Party	Release the Bats
20	The Undertones	Get Over You
21	The Specials	Ghost Town
22	Scritti Politti	The Sweetest Girl
23	The Jam	Going Underground
24	Stiff Little Fingers	Johnny Was
25	Theatre of Hate	Legion
26	Public Image Ltd.	Public Image
27	Killing Joke	Requiem
28	Killing Joke	Follow the Leaders
29	Heaven 17	(We Don't Need This) Fascist Groove Thang
30	The Fall	Fiery Jack
31	The Ruts	In A Rut
32	Stiff Little Fingers	Suspect Device
33	The Fall	How I Wrote 'Elastic Man'
34	Laurie Anderson	O Superman
35	Siouxsie & the Banshees	Jigsaw Feeling
36	B-Movie	Remembrance Day
37	Siouxsie & the Banshees	Israel
38	Sex Pistols	God Save the Queen
39	Pigbag	Papa's Got a Brand New Pigbag
40	Siouxsie & the Banshees	Icon
41	The Only Ones	Another Girl, Another Planet
42	Dead Kennedys	California Uber Alles
43	Joy Division	Twenty-Four Hours
44	Joy Division	Isolation
45	Killing Joke	Psyche
46	Echo & the Bunnymen	Over the Wall
47	The Fall	Lie Dream of a Casino Soul
48	New Order	Procession
49	Siouxsie & the Banshees	Switch
50	Altered Images	Happy Birthday
51	Joy Division	She's Lost Control

52	Bauhaus	Bela Lugosi's Dead
53	Magazine	Shot By Both Sides
54	New Order	In a Lonely Place
55	Anti-Pasti	No Government
56	The Fall	Totally Wired
57	The Specials	Gangsters
58	The Fire Engines	Candy Skin
59	Sex Pistols	Pretty Vacant
60	Siouxsie & the Banshees	Hong Kong Garden

1982 (Part 1 – 1982)

1	New Order	Temptation
2	Robert Wyatt	Shipbuilding
3	Grandmaster Flash & the Furious 5	The Message
4	Echo & the Bunnymen	The Back of Love
5	Tears For Fears	Mad World
6	The Clash	Straight to Hell
7	Wah!	Story of the Blues
8	Theatre of Hate	Do You Believe in the West World
9	Artery	Into the Garden
10	Wild Swans	Revolutionary Spirit
11	The Jam	Town Called Malice
12	Yazoo	Only You
13	Scritti Politti	Faithless
14	The Associates	Party Fears Two
14	Bauhaus	Ziggy Stardust
16	Siouxsie & the Banshees	Fireworks
17	New Order	Hurt
18	Scritti Politti	Asylums in Jerusalem
19	Dexy's Midnight Runners	Come On Eileen
20	Killing Joke	Empire Song
21	The Farmer's Boys	Whatever is he Like?
22	China Crisis	African and White
23	Siouxsie & the Banshees	Slow Dive

24	Aztec Camera	Pillar To Post
25	The Cure	The Hanging Garden
26	The Clash	Should I Stay Or Should I Go?
27	The Clash	Know Your Rights
28	The Cure	The Figurehead
29	Psychedelic Furs	Love My Way
30	Simple Minds	Promised You A Miracle
31	The Redskins	Peasant Army
32	Simple Minds	Someone Somewhere (in Summertime)
33	The Cure	A Strange Day
34	Blancmange	Living on the Ceiling
35	Blancmange	Feel Me
36	Musical Youth	Pass the Dutchie
37	Cocteau Twins	Wax and Wane
38	Serious Drinking	Love on the Terraces
39	The Jam	The Bitterest Pill (I Ever Had To Swallow)
40	The Clash	Rock the Casbah
41	The Passage	XOYO
42	Chameleons	In Shreds
43	Weekend	A View From Her Room
44	Shambeko! Say Wah!	Remember
45	Simple Minds	Glittering Prize
46	Bauhaus	Third Uncle
47	The Higsons	Conspiracy
48	Action Pact	Suicide Bag
49	Siouxsie & the Banshees	Melt!
50	The Farmer's Boys	I Think I Need Help
51	The Stranglers	Strange Little Girl
52	Josef K	The Missionary
53	Gregory Isaacs	Night Nurse
54	Everything But the Girl	Night and Day
55	The Associates	Club Country
56	The Stranglers	Golden Brown
57	Theatre of Hate	The Hop

58	The Fall	Look, Know
59	Captain Sensible	Happy Talk
60	Yazoo	Don't Go

1982 (Part 2 – All Time)

1	Sex Pistols	Anarchy in the UK
2	Joy Division	Atmosphere
3	Joy Division	Love Will Tear Us Apart
4	Joy Division	New Dawn Fades
5	The Cure	A Forest
6	New Order	Ceremony
7	Joy Division	Decades
8	The Undertones	Teenage Kicks
9	Bauhaus	Bela Lugosi's Dead
10	The Clash	White Man in Hammersmith Palais
11	The Jam	Down in the Tube Station at Midnight
12	Joy Division	Dead Souls
13	The Damned	New Rose
14	Dead Kennedys	Holiday in Cambodia
15	Siouxsie & the Banshees	Israel
16	Stiff Little Fingers	Alternative Ulster
17	The Jam	Going Underground
18	New Order	Temptation
19	The Clash	Complete Control
20	Public Image Ltd.	Public Image
21	Altered Images	Dead Pop Stars
22	Echo & the Bunnymen	Over the Wall
23	Joy Division	Twenty-Four Hours
24	The Only Ones	Another Girl, Another Planet
25	Sex Pistols	God Save the Queen
26	Joy Division	Transmission
27	Scritti Politti	The 'Sweetest' Girl
28	The Birthday Party	Release the Bats

29	Stiff Little Fingers	Johnny Was
30	New Order	Procession
31	Stiff Little Fingers	Suspect Device
32	Killing Joke	Requiem
33	Theatre of Hate	Legion
34	Killing Joke	Psyche
35	The Ruts	In A Rut
36	The Undertones	Get Over You
37	Sex Pistols	Holidays in the Sun
38	Joy Division	Isolation
39	Siouxsie & the Banshees	Jigsaw Feeling
40	The Clash	Armagideon Time
41	Joy Division	She's Lost Control
42	Siouxsie & the Banshees	Switch
43	The Specials	Ghost Town
44	Sex Pistols	Pretty Vacant
45	Siouxsie & the Banshees	Icon
46	Siouxsie & the Banshees	Hong Kong Garden
47	Magazine	Shot By Both Sides
48	Joy Division	The Eternal
49=	Laurie Anderson	O Superman
49=	The Damned	Love Song

1983

1	New Order	Blue Monday
2	The Smiths	This Charming Man
3	New Order	Age of Consent
4	This Mortal Coil	Song to the Siren
5	Cocteau Twins	Musette and Drums
6	The Smiths	Reel Around the Fountain
7	Billy Bragg	A New England
8	The Fall	Eat Y'self Fitter
9	The Smiths	Hand in Glove
10	Naturalites	Picture on the Wall

11	The Red Guitars	Good Technology
12	Public Image Ltd	This is Not a Love Song
13	X-Mal Deutschland	Incubus Succubus
14	Cocteau Twins	Sugar Hiccup
15	The Cure	Lovecats
16	Cocteau Twins	From the Flagstones
17	Echo & the Bunnymen	Never Stop
18	New Order	Your Silent Face
19	Sisters of Mercy	Temple of Love
20	Siouxsie & the Banshees	Dear Prudence
21	The Fall	The Man Whose Head Expanded
22	Echo & the Bunnymen	The Cutter
23	The Assembly	Never Never
24	The Imposter	Pills and Soap
25	New Order	Leave Me Alone
26	10,000 Maniacs	My Mother the War
27	Sisters of Mercy	Alice
28	Cocteau Twins	Peppermint Pig
29	Aztec Camera	Oblivious
30	The Redskins	Lean On Me
31	The Chameleons	Second Skin
32	X-Mal Deutschland	Qual
33	The Smiths	Handsome Devil
34	Tools You Can Trust	Working and Shopping
35	The Fall	Kicker Conspiracy
36	The Luddites	Doppelganger
37	Sophie and Peter Johnston	Television/Satellite
38	Cocteau Twins	Hitherto
39	S.P.K	Metal Dance
40	The Fall	Wings
41	U2	New Year's Day
42	The Danse Society	Somewhere
43	The Birthday Party	Deep in the Woods
44	Cabaret Voltaire	Just Fascination
45	New Order	The Village
46	The Birthday Party	Sonny's Burning

47	Strawberry Switchblade	Trees and Flowers
48	Elvis Costello	Shipbuilding
49	The Cure	The Walk
50	Tom Robinson	War Baby

1984

....

1	The Smiths	How Soon is Now?
2	Cocteau Twins	Pearly Dewdrops Drop
3	The Men They Couldn't Hang	Green Fields of France
4	Cocteau Twins	Spangle Maker
5	Mighty Wah!	Come Back
6	The Membranes	Spike Milligan's Tape Recorder
7	New Order	Thieves Like Us
8	Sisters of Mercy	Walk Away
9	The Fall	Lay of the Land
10	The Redskins	Keep On Keepin' On
11	Nick Cave and the Bad Seeds	Saint Huck
12	New Order	Lonesome Tonight
13	Billy Bragg	Between the Wars
14	The Smiths	Nowhere Fast
15	Sisters of Mercy	Emma
16	Cocteau Twins	Ivo
17	The Smiths	What Difference Does it Make?
18	The Fall	Creep
19	Echo & the Bunnymen	The Killing Moon
20	New Order	Murder
21	This Mortal Coil	Kangaroo
22	Cocteau Twins	Donimo
23	The Smiths	William, It Was Really Nothing
24	The Smiths	Heaven Knows I'm Miserable Now
25	Frankie Goes To Hollywood	Two Tribes
26	Unknown Cases	Masimbabele

27	The Very Things	The Bushes Scream While My Daddy Prunes
28	The Smiths	Please, Please, Please, Let Me Get What I Want
29	Billy Bragg	The Saturday Boy
30	The Cult	Spiritwalker
31	Propaganda	Dr Mabuse
32	Yeah Yeah Noh	Bias Binding
33	This Mortal Coil	Another Day
34	Berntholer	My Suitor
35	Robert Wyatt	Biko
36	The Smiths	Reel Around the Fountain
37	The Jesus & Mary Chain	Upside Down
38	Cocteau Twins	Pandora
39	Flesh For Lulu	Subterraneans
40	Cocteau Twins	Beatrix
41	Special AKA	Free Nelson Mandela
42	Frank Chickens	Blue Canary
43	New Model Army	Vengeance
44	The Fall	No Bulbs
45	The Pogues	Dark Streets of London
46	Hard Corps	Dirty
47	Echo & the Bunnymen	Thorn of Crowns
48	Bronski Beat	Small Town Boy
49	Cocteau Twins	Pepper Tree
50	Working Week	Venceremos

1985

1	The Jesus & Mary Chain	Never Understand
2	The Jesus & Mary Chain	Just Like Honey
3	The Fall	Cruiser's Creek
4	The Cult	She Sells Sanctuary
5	Cocteau Twins	Aikea-Guinea
6	Chumbawamba	Revolution
7	Felt	Primitive Painters

8	The Smiths	The Boy With the Thorn in His Side
9	New Order	Perfect Kiss
10	The Housemartins	Flag Day
11	The Men They Couldn't Hang	Ironmasters
12	The Jesus & Mary Chain	You Trip Me Up
13	The Pogues	Sally Maclennane
14	The Three Johns	Death of the European
15	The Wedding Present	Go Out and Get 'em Boy!
16	New Order	Love Vigilantes
17	The Shop Assistants	All That Ever Mattered
18	New Order	Sub-Culture
19	The Woodentops	Move Me
20	The Pogues	A Pair of Brown Eyes
21	Echo & the Bunnymen	Bring on the Dancing Horses
22	That Petrol Emotion	V2
23	The Fall	Spoilt Victorian Child
24	New Order	Sunrise
25	The Pogues	I'm A Man You Don't Meet Every Day
26	Rose of Avalanche	L.A. Rain
27	The Cure	In Between Days
28	James	Hymn From a Village
29	The Smiths	The Headmaster Ritual
30	The Age of Chance	Motor City
31	The Smiths	That Joke Isn't Funny Anymore
32	The Smiths	Meat is Murder
33	The Fall	Gut of the Quantifier
34	Beloved	100 Words (session)
35	Nick Cave & the Bad Seeds	Tupelo
36	Sisters of Mercy	Marian
37	The Vibes	I'm in Pittsburgh & It's Raining
38	Prefab Sprout	Faron Young (Truckin' Mix)
39	The Fall	Couldn't Get Ahead
40	Billy Bragg	Between the Wars

41	The Smiths	Well I Wonder
42	The Fall	L.A.
43	Sisters of Mercy	Some Kind of Stranger
44	Primal Scream	It Happens
45	New Order	Face Up
46	Hüsker Dü	Makes No Sense At All
47	Robert Wyatt	The Wind of Change
48	The Woodentops	Well Well Well
49	One Thousand Violins	Like One Thousand Violins
50	The Shop Assistants	All Day Long
51	James	If Things Were Perfect
52	Del Amitri	Hammering Heart
53	Conflict	Mighty & Superior
54	Siouxsie & the Banshees	Cities In Dust
55	The Fall	Rollin' Danny
56	Billy Bragg	Days Like These
57	The Smiths	Barbarism Begins At Home
58	Big Flame	All the Irish Must Go To Heaven
59	10,000 Maniacs	Can't Ignore the Train
60	Cabaret Voltaire	I Want You
61	The Smiths	Shakespeare's Sister
62	Big Flame	Man of Few Syllables
63	Cocteau Twins	Quisquose
64	The Pogues	And the Band Played Waltzing Matilda
65	Bogshed	Hand Me Down Father
66	New Model Army	No Rest
67	The Cure	Close To Me
68	The Triffids	Field of Glass
69	10,000 Maniacs	Just as the Tide Was A-Flowing
70	That Petrol Emotion	Keen

1986

1	The Smiths	There is a Light That Never Goes Out
2	The Age of Chance	Kiss
3	The Fall	Mr Pharmacist
4	Primal Scream	Velocity Girl
5	The Smiths	Panic
6	The Smiths	I Know It's Over
7	The Smiths	The Queen is Dead
8	The Shop Assistants	Safety Net
9	The Jesus & Mary Chain	Some Candy Talking
10	The Fall	US 80s–90s
11	The Smiths	Ask
12	The Smiths	Bigmouth Strikes Again
13	The Weather Prophets	Almost Prayed
14	Half Man Half Biscuit	Trumpton Riots
15	The Fall	Living Too Late
16	The Wedding Present	Once More
17	The Soup Dragons	Hang Ten!
18	The Wedding Present	This Boy Can Wait
19	The Bodines	Therese
20	The Fall	Bournemouth Runner
21	Cocteau Twins	Love's Easy Tears
22	The Primitives	Really Stupid
23	The Pastels	Truck Train Tractor
24	Billy Bragg	Levi Stubbs' Tears
25	The Soup Dragons	Whole Wide World
26	The Fall	Realm of Dusk (session)
27	Age of Chance	Bible of the Beats
28	The Wedding Present	You Should Always Keep in Touch With Your Friends
29	That Petrol Emotion	It's a Good Thing
30	The Very Things	This is Motortown
31	We've Got a Fuzzbox	Rules & Regulations
32	The The	Heartland

33	Freiwillige Selbstokontrolle	I Wish I Could Sprechen Sie Deutsch
34	The Mighty Lemon Drops	Like an Angel
35	The Smiths	Cemetry Gates
36	The Wedding Present	Felicity (session)
37	The Fall	Lucifer Over Lancashire (Theology Mix)
38	Cocteau Twins	Those Eyes, That Mouth
39	Half Man Half Biscuit	Dickie Davies Eyes
40	Elvis Costello	I Want You
41	Billy Bragg	Greetings to the New Brunette
42	The Flatmates	I Could Be in Heaven
43	The Shop Assistants	I Don't Want to Be Friends With You
44	Mighty Mighty	Is There Anyone Out There?
45	Nick Cave & the Bad Seeds	By the Time I Get to Phoenix
46	Colourbox	The Official Colourbox World Cup Theme
47	Camper Van Beethoven	Take the Skinheads Bowling
48	The Fall	Dktr Faustus
49	The Mission	Serpent's Kiss
50	The Pogues	The Body of an American

1987

1	The Sugarcubes	Birthday
2	The Fall	Australians in Europe
3	The Wedding Present	Everyone Thinks He Looks Daft
4	That Petrol Emotion	Big Decision
5	The Smiths	Last Night I Dreamt That Somebody Loved Me
6	The Wedding Present	My Favourite Dress
7	New Order	True Faith
8	The Wedding Present	A Million Miles
9	The Fall	Hit the North
10	The Wedding Present	Anyone Can Make A Mistake
11	I, Ludicrous	Preposterous Tales

12	The Smiths	Stop Me if You Think You've Heard This One Before
13	Sonic Youth	Schizophrenia
14	Public Enemy	Rebel Without a Pause
15	The Smiths	Girlfriend in a Coma
16	The Jesus & Mary Chain	April Skies
17	Barmy Army	Sharp as a Needle
18	Big Black	Colombian Necktie
19	The Primitives	Stop Killing Me
20	Cud	You Sexy Thing
21	Smiths	Paint a Vulgar Picture
22	Motorcycle Boy	Big Rock Candy Mountain
23	The Smiths	Sweet and Tender Hooligan
24	The Smiths	Half a Person
25	The Smiths	Death of a Disco Dancer
26	The Fall	Athlete Cured (Session)
27	Eric B & Rakim	Paid In Full (Coldcut Remix)
28	The Railway Children	Brighter
29	The Smiths	I Won't Share You
30	The Bhundu Boys	My Foolish Heart
31	The Wedding Present	Getting Nowhere Fast
32	Prince	Sign O' the Times
33	James Taylor Quartet	Blow Up!
34	The Smiths	Sheila Take a Bow
35	McCarthy	Frans Hals
36	Eric B & Rakim	I Know You Got Soul
37	Sonic Youth	(I Got A) Catholic Block
38	Public Enemy	You're Gonna Get Yours
39	The Jesus & Mary Chain	Kill Surf City
40	The Smiths	I Started Something I Couldn't Finish
41	The Jesus & Mary Chain	Nine Million Rainy Days
42	Big Black	L Dopa
43	New Order	1963
44	Butthole Surfers	22 Going On 23
45	The Smiths	Shoplifters of the World Unite
46	M/A/R/R/S	Pump Up the Volume

47	Colorblind James Experience	I'm Considering A Move to Memphis
48	The Gun Club	Breaking Hands
49	Beatmasters & the Cookie Crew	Rok Da House
50	Talulah Gosh	Talulah Gosh

1988

1	The House of Love	Destroy the Heart
2	The Wedding Present	Nobody's Twisting Your Arm
3	The Jesus & Mary Chain	Sidewalking
4	The Wedding Present	Take Me (I'm Yours) (session)
5	Dinosaur Jr	Freak Scene
6	My Bloody Valentine	You Made Me Realise
7	The Pixies	Gigantic
8	The Wedding Present	Why Are You Being So Reasonable Now?
9	The House of Love	Christine
10	Nick Cave & the Bad Seeds	The Mercy Seat
11	Inspiral Carpets	Keep the Circle Around
12	Morrissey	Everyday is Like Sunday
13	Morrissey	Suedehead
14	The Fall	Cab It Up
15	Wedding Present	I'm Not Always So Stupid
16	The Fall	Bremen Nacht
17	My Bloody Valentine	Feed Me With Your Kiss
18	The House of Love	Love In a Car
19	Sonic Youth	Teenage Riot
20	The Sugarcubes	Deus
21	Robert Lloyd & the New Four Seasons	Something Nice
22	Morrissey	Late Night, Maudlin Street
23	Morrissey	Disappointed
24	The Fall	Big New Prinz
25	Billy Bragg	Waiting for the Great Leap Forwards

26	Cocteau Twins	Carolyn's Fingers
27	The Fall	Kurious Oranj
28	Overlord X	14 Days in May
29	Sonic Youth	Silver Rocket
30	The Pixies	Where is My Mind?
31	Mudhoney	Sweet Young Thing Ain't Sweet No More
32	Spit	Road Pizza
33	James	What For
34	The Pooh Sticks	On Tape (session)
35	Stump	Charlton Heston
36	The Fall	Jerusalem
37	Shalawambe	Samora Machel (session)
38	McCarthy	Should the Bible Be Banned
39	The Pixies	River Euphrates
40	The Fall	Guest Informant
41	Loop	Collision
42	The Flatmates	Shimmer
43	Mega City Four	Miles Apart
44	New Order	Fine Time
45	The Pixies	Bone Machine
46	The Primitives	Crash
47	The Darling Buds	Shame On You
48	Happy Mondays	Wrote For Luck
49	The Wedding Present	Don't Laugh
50	Public Enemy	Night of the Living Baseheads

1989

1	The Sundays	Can't Be Sure
2	The Wedding Present	Kennedy
3	The Pixies	Debaser
4	Happy Mondays	WFL
5	The Pixies	Monkey Gone to Heaven
6	The Stone Roses	I Am the Resurrection

7	The Stone Roses	She Bangs the Drums
8	James	Sit Down
9	Inspiral Carpets	Joe
10	The House of Love	I Don't Know Why I Love You
11	The Pale Saints	Sight of You
12	Dinosaur Jr	Just Like Heaven
13	The Jesus & Mary Chain	Blues From a Gun
14	The Wedding Present	Take Me (I'm Yours)
15	Cud	Only a Prawn in Whitby
16	Mudhoney	You Got It (Keep It Outta My Face)
17	The Stone Roses	Made of Stone
18	Morrissey	The Last of the Famous International Playboys
19	The Wedding Present	Brassneck
20	Morrissey	Ouija Board, Ouija Board
21	Inspiral Carpets	Find Out Why
22	808 State	Pacific State
23	The Stone Roses	Fool's Gold
24	Wedding Present	Bewitched
25	The Pale Saints	She Rides the Waves
26	The Field Mice	Sensitive
27	New Order	Vanishing Point
28	Birdland	Hollow Heart
29	The Stone Roses	I Wanna Be Adored
30	The Telescopes	Perfect Needle
31	Bob	Convenience
32	Jesus Jones	Info Freako
33	Spacemen 3	Hypnotised
34	De La Soul	Eye Know
35	Inspiral Carpets	So This is How it Feels (session)
36	The Pixies	Wave of Mutilation
37	The Pixies	Here Comes Your Man
38	The Fall	Dead Beat Descendant
39	DubSex	Swerve
40	Birdland	Paradise

41	Galaxie 500	Don't Let Our Youth Go to Waste
42	Senseless Things	Too Much Kissing
43	The Pixies	Dead
44	Snuff	Not Listening
45	The Wedding Present	What Have I Said Now?
46	The Popguns	Landslide
47	Morrissey	Interesting Drug
48	The Family Cat	Tom Verlaine
49	Inspiral Carpets	Directing Traffic
50	Inspiral Carpets	She Comes in the Fall

1990

1	The Fall	Bill is Dead
2	My Bloody Valentine	Soon
3	Ride	Dreams Burn Down
4	Ride	Like a Daydream
5	Sonic Youth	Tunic (Song For Karen)
6	Paris Angels	(All On You) Perfume
7	The Wedding Present	Make Me Smile (Come Up & See Me)
8	Happy Mondays	Step On
9	The Wedding Present	Corduroy
10	The Orb	Loving You (session)
11	Teenage Fanclub	Everything Flows
12	Would-Be's	I'm Hardly Ever Wrong
13	The Lemonheads	Different Drum
14	New Fast Automatic Daffodils	Big
15	The Fall	White Lightning
16	Morrissey	November Spawned a Monster
17	The Charlatans	The Only One I Know
18	The Wedding Present	Don't Talk, Just Kiss
19	Nick Cave	The Ship Song
20	The Wedding Present	Heather (session)
21	The Boo Radleys	Kaleidoscope

22	The Wedding Present	Crawl
23	Nirvana	Sliver
24	The Pixies	The Happening
25	Ride	Taste
26	Ned's Atomic Dustbin	Kill Your Television
27	Lush	Sweetness & Light
28	The Charlatans	Polar Bear
29	Dinosaur Jr	The Wagon
30	The Fall	Blood Outta Stone
31	The Pixies	Velouria
32	Happy Mondays	Kinky Afro
33	Fatima Mansions	Blues For Ceaucescu
34	Shamen	Pro-Gen
35	The Fall	Telephone Thing
36	The Sundays	Here's Where the Story Ends
37	Spiritualized	Any Way That You Want Me
38	Babes in Toyland	House
39	The Wedding Present	Dalliance
40	Sonic Youth	Kool Thing
41	The Fall	Chicago, Now!
42	The Orb	Little Fluffy Clouds
43	Teenage Fanclub	God Knows It's True
44	Deee-Lite	Groove is in the Heart
45	Bastro	Nothing Special
46	The Farm	Stepping Stone
47	The Farm	Groovy Train
48	The Pixies	Alison
49	The Pixies	Dig For Fire
50	Inspiral Carpets	Beast Inside

1991

1	Nirvana	Smells Like Teen Spirit
2	PJ Harvey	Dress
3	Curve	Ten Little Girls
4	The Fall	Edinburgh Man

5	Teenage Fanclub	Star Sign
6	Teenage Fanclub	The Concept
7	Hole	Burn Black
8	The Wedding Present	Dalliance
9	The Fall	A Lot of Wind
10	Hole	Teenage Whore
11	Primal Scream	Higher Than the Sun
12	The Wedding Present	Dare
13	Gallon Drunk	Some Fools Mess
14	The Wedding Present	Fleshworld
15	Catherine Wheel	Black Metallic
16	Nirvana	Drain You
17	Moose	Suzanne
18	Babes in Toyland	Hansel & Gretel
19	The Boo Radleys	Finest Kiss
20	Slowdive	Catch the Breeze
21	Foreheads in a Fishtank	Happy Shopper
22	The Wedding Present	Rotterdam
23	Slint	Good Morning, Captain
24	The Fall	High Tension Line
25	Nirvana	Lithium
26	The Pixies	Planet of Sound
27	Smashing Pumpkins	Siva
28	70 Gwen Party	Auto Killer UK
29	Billy Bragg	Sexuality
30	Babes in Toyland	Catatonic
31	Babes in Toyland	Laugh My Head Off
32	The Wedding Present	Octopussy
33	Chapterhouse	Pearl
34	Pavement	Summer Babe
35	The Fall	The War Against Intelligence
36	Teenage Fanclub	Like A Virgin
37	My Bloody Valentine	To Here Knows Where
38	Curve	No Escape From Heaven
39	Babes in Toyland	Primus
40	Electronic	Get the Message
41	The Fall	The Mixer

42	Babes in Toyland	Ripe
43	The Fall	So What About It?
44	Th' Faith Healers	Gorgeous Blue Flower in My Garden
45	The Field Mice	Missing the Moon
46	The Pixies	Motorway to Roswell
47	The Pixies	Bird Dream of the Olympus Mons
48	Nirvana	Breed
49	Mercury Rev	Car Wash Hair
50	Bongwater	Nick Cave Doll

1992

1	Bang Bang Machine	Geek Love
2	PJ Harvey	Sheela-Na-Gig
3	Ministry	Jesus Built My Hotrod
4	The Wedding Present	Come Play With Me
5	The Fall	The Legend of Xanadu
6	The Fall	Free Range
7	Sonic Youth	Youth Against Fascism
8	Pavement	Trigger Cut
9	Babes In Toyland	Bruise Violets
10	Pavement	Here
11	Future Sound of London	Papua New Guinea
12	The Fall	Ed's Babe
13	The Jesus & Mary Chain	Reverence
14	The Wedding Present	Flying Saucer
15	Suede	The Drowners
16	Sugar	Changes
17	Sonic Youth	Sugar Kane
18	The Wedding Present	Silver Shorts
19	The Wedding Present	Love Slave
20	The Orb	Blue Room
21	Sugar	A Good Idea
22	Babes in Toyland	Hansel & Gretel
23	Sonic Youth	100%

24	The Wedding Present	Blue Eyes
25	Dr Devious	Cyber Dream
26	Sonic Youth	Theresa's Sound World
27	Pond	Young Splendour
28	Drop Nineteens	Wynnona
29	Datblygu	Popeth
30	Disposable Heroes of Hiphoprisy	The Language of Violence
31	The Frank & Walters	Happy Bus Man
32	Arcwelder	Favour
33	Therapy?	Teethgrinder
34	The Fall	Kimble
35	Pavement	In the Mouth a Desert
36	Love Cup	Tearing Water
37	Pavement	Summer Babe
38	Disposable Heroes of Hiphoprisy	Television the Drug of a Nation
39	The Boo Radleys	Lazarus
40	Ride	Leave Them All Behind
41	The Wedding Present	Sticky
42	Pavement	Circa 1762
43	Drag Racing Underground	On the Road Again
44	KLF & Extreme Noise Terror	3AM Eternal
45	Buffalo Tom	Taillights Fade
46	The Wedding Present	Falling
47	Pavement	Conduit For Sale
48	Sugar	Helpless
49	The Verve	All in the Mind
50	The Fall	The Birmingham School of Business School

1993

1	Chumbawamba & Credit to the Nation	Enough is Enough
2	Madder Rose	Swim
3	Huggy Bear	Her Jazz

4	PJ Harvey	Rid of Me
5	Stereolab	French Disco
6	Voodoo Queens	Supermodel Superficial
7	Sebadoh	Soul & Fire
8	The Breeders	Cannonball
9	Palace Brothers	Ohio River Boat Song
10	The Eggs	Government Administrator
11	The Fall	Why Are People Grudgeful
12	Credit to the Nation & Chumbawamba	Hear No Bullshit
13	New Order	Regret
14	Pulp	Razzamatazz
15	PJ Harvey	50ft Queenie
16	The New Bad Things	You Suck
17	Cornershop	England's Dreaming
18	PJ Harvey	Wang Dang Doodle
19	The Fall	Lost in Music
20	The Fall	Glam Racket
21	Senser	Eject
22	The Fall	I'm Going to Spain
23	Archers of Loaf	Web in Front
24	Credit to the Nation	Call It What You Want
25	Hole	Olympia
26	The Fall	Service
27	Tindersticks	Raindrops
28	Chumbawamba	Timebomb
29	The Fall	Ladybird (Green Grass)
30	Tindersticks	Marbles
31	Radiohead	Creep
32	PJ Harvey	Naked Cousin
33	Heavenly	At A Girl
34	J Church	Good Judge of Character
35	The Boo Radleys	Barney & Me
36	Madder Rose	Beautiful John
37	Tindersticks	City Sickness
38	Elastica	Stutter
39	Stereolab	Jenny Ondioline
40	Nirvana	Scentless Apprentice

41	The Fall	A Past Gone Mad
42	Dinosaur Jr	Get Me
43	The Fall	Behind the Counter
44	Madder Rose	Lights Go Down
45	Nirvana	Rape Me
46	Pulp	Lipgloss
47	Hole	Beautiful Son
48	The Fall	It's a Curse
49	Trans-Global Underground	Syrius B
50	The Fall	War

1994

1	Inspiral Carpets (featuring Mark E Smith)	I Want You
2	The Fall	Hey Student
3	Veruca Salt	Seether
4	Elastica	Connection
5	Supergrass	Caught by the Fuzz
6	LSG	Hearts
7	Elastica	Waking Up
8	Portishead	Sour Times
9	Stereolab	Ping Pong
10	Done Lying Down	Just a Misdemeanour
11	H Foundation	Laika
12	Ash	Jack Names the Planets
13	Pulp	Do You Remember the First Time?
14	Pavement	Range Life
15	The Wedding Present	Swimming Pools, Movie Stars
16	Sebadoh	Rebound
17	Hole	Miss World
18	Shellac	Crow
19	Madder Rose	The Car Song
20	Sleeper	Delicious
21	Pulp	Common People

22	Pavement	Gold Soundz
23	Pulp	Babies
24	Shellac	The Dog & Pony Show
25	Mazzy Star	Fade Into You
26	That Dog	One Summer Night
27	Nirvana	The Man Who Sold the World
28	Ash	Uncle Pat
29	Sabres of Paradise	Wilmot
30	Wedding Present	Click Click
31	Orbital	Are We Here? (Industry Standard Mix)
32	Beck	Loser
33	Ash	Petrol
34	Pavement	Cut Your Hair
35	Madder Rose	Panic On
36	Salt Tank	Charged Up
37	The Wedding Present	So Long Baby
38	The Fall	City Dweller
39	The Wedding Present	Spangle
40	Nirvana	Where Did You Sleep Last Night?
41	The Fall	M5
42	Elastica	Line Up
43	Underworld	Dirty Epic
44	Nirvana	About a Girl
45	Hole	Doll Parts
46	ROC	Girl With a Crooked Eye
47	Sonic Youth	Superstar
48	Sleeper	Swallow
49	Tuscadero	Angel in a Half Shirt
50	Trans-Global Underground	Taal Zaman

1995

| 1 | Pulp | Common People |
| 2 | Pulp | Sorted For E's & Wizz |

3	The Wedding Present	Sucker
4	Ash	Girl From Mars
5	Dreadzone	Zion Youth
6	Ash	Kung Fu
7	The Fall	Feeling Numb
8	Pulp	I-Spy
9	Dreadzone	Maximum
10	Long Fin Killie & Mark E Smith	Heads of Dead Surfers
11	PJ Harvey	Send His Love to Me
12	Pulp	Mis-shapes
13	Supergrass	Alright
14	Zion Train	Dance of Life
15	The Bluetones	Bluetonic
16	Dreadzone	Fight the Power
17	PJ Harvey	Down By the Water
18	Catatonia	Bleed
19	Gorky's Zygotic Mynci	If Fingers Were Xylophones
20	Elastica	All Nighter
21	The Bluetones	Slight Return
22	Tricky	Black Steel
23	Dreadzone	Little Britain
24	The Fall	Don't Call Me Darling
25	Tindersticks	My Sister
26	Dick Dale	Nitro
27	Pulp	Disco 2000
28	Hole	Violet
29	Flaming Stars	Kiss Tomorrow Goodbye
30	The Fall	Bonkers in Phoenix
31	Pulp	Underwear
32	Spare Snare	Bugs
33	Stereolab	Pop Quiz
34	PJ Harvey	To Bring You My Love
35	Dreadzone	Captain Dread
36	Cornershop	6am Jullander Shere
37	Billy Bragg	Northern Industrial Town
38	Van Basten	King of the Death Posture
39	Solar Race	Not Here

40	Pavement	Father to a Sister of Thought
41	Leftfield	Afro Left
42	Harvey's Rabbit	Is This What You Call Change?
43	Ash	Angel Interceptor
44	Dose (with Mark E Smith)	Plug Myself In
45	Garbage	Vow
46	Dave Clarke	Red Three
47	Bis	School Disco
48	Dreadzone	Life, Love & Unity
49	The Fall	The Joke
50	Safe Deposit	You Can't

1996

1	Kenickie	Come Out 2 Nite
2	Arab Strap	First Big Weekend
3	The Delgados	Under Canvas Under Wraps
4	Kenickie	Punka
5	Underworld	Born Slippy
6	The Fall	Cheetham Hill
7	Orbital	The Box
8	Gorky's Zygotic Mynci	Patio Song
9	Sweeney	Why?
10	Helen Love	Girl About Town
11	Stereolab	Cybele's Reverie
12	Billy Bragg	Brickbat
13	The Fall	The Chiselers
14	Bis	Kandy Pop
15	Baby Bird	Goodnight
16	The Fall	Hostile
17	Polly Harvey & John Parrish	That Was My Veil
18	Flaming Stars	10 Feet Tall
19	Trembling Blue Stars	Abba on the Jukebox
20	Stereolab	Fluorescences
21	Tortoise	DJED
22	Jon Spencer Blues Explosion	2 Kindsa Love

Festive 50s

23	Polly Harvey & John Parrish	Taut
24	Quickspace	Friend
25	Dave Clarke	No One's Driving
26	AC Acoustics	Stunt Girl
27	Dick Dale	Nitrous
28	Belle & Sebastian	The State I'm In
29	Aphex Twin	Girl/Boy
30	Force & Stars	Fireworks
31	White Town	Your Woman
32	Zion Train	Babylon's Burning
33	Calvin Party	Lies, Lies & Government
34	Broadcast	The Book Lovers
35	DJ Shadow	Stem
36	The Wedding Present	2, 3, Go
37	The Prodigy	Firestarter
38	Ash	Oh Yeah
39	Placebo	Teenage Angst
40	Broadcast	Living Room
41	Tiger	The Race
42	Manic Street Preachers	A Design For Life
43	Half Man Half Biscuit	Paintball's Coming Home
44	Soul Bossa	Sore Loser
45	Urusei Yatsura	Kewpies Like Watermelon
46	The Wedding Present	Go Man Go
47	Orbital	Out There Somewhere
48	Flaming Stars	The Face on the Bar Room Floor
49	Super Furry Animals	God Show Me Magic
50	Stereolab	Les Yper-Sound

1997

1	Cornershop	Brimful of Asha
2	Mogwai	New Paths to Helicon
3	Helen Love	Does Your Heart Go Boom?
4	Period Pains	Spice Girls (Who Do You Think You Are?)

5	Belle & Sebastian	Lazy Line Painter Jane
6	Novac	Rapunzel
7	The Fall	Inch
8	Daft Punk	Rollin' & Scratchin'
9	Clinic	IPC Sub-editors Dictate Our Youth
10	David Holmes	Don't Die Yet (Arab Strap Mix)
11	Blur	Song 2
12	Belle & Sebastian	Dog on Wheels
13	Hydroplane	Cross the Atlantic
14	Stereolab & Nurse With Wound	Simple Headphone Mind
15	Bette Davies & the Balconettes	Shergar
16	Arab Strap	Hey! Fever
17	The Fall	I'm A Mummy
18	Spiritualized	Ladies & Gentlemen We Are Floating in Space
19	AC Acoustics	I Messiah Am Jailer
20	Stereolab	Fluorescences
21	The Hitchers	Strachan
22	Bis	Sweetshop Avenger
23	Synchro Goldfish	Dandelion Milk Summer
24	Prolapse	Autocade
25	Dream City Film Club	If I Die I Die
26	Stereolab	Mismodular
27	The Delgados	Pull the Wires From the Wall
28	Propellerheads	Velvet Pants
29	Highbirds	Seventeen
30	Prolapse	Slash/Oblique
31	Angelica	Teenage Girl Crush

1998

1	The Delgados	Pull the Wires From the Wall
2	Mogwai	Xmas Steps
3	Belle & Sebastian	The Boy With the Arab Strap
4	Ten Benson	The Claw

5	Tuesday	Unworldly
6	The Cuban Boys	Oh My God They Killed Kenny
7	Bis	Eurodisco
8	Pulp	This is Hardcore
9	The Delgados	Everything Goes Around the Water
10	Helen Love	Long Live the UK Music Scene
11	The Jesus & Mary Chain	Cracking Up
12	Daniel Johnston	Dream Scream
13	Clinic	Cement Mixer
14	Badly Drawn Boy	I Need a Sign
15	Cinerama	Kerry Kerry
16	Plone	Plock
17	L'Augmentation	Soleil
18	Boards of Canada	Aquarius
19	Solex	Solex All Lickety Spit
20	Evolution Control Committee	Copyright Violation for the Nation
21	Massive Attack	Teardrop
22	Spiritualized	Oh Happy Day
23	Solex	One Louder Solex
24	Melys	Lemming, Chameleon of Feelings
25	Half Man Half Biscuit	Turn a Blind Eye
26	Belle & Sebastian	Sleep the Clock Around
27	Clinic	Monkey On Your Back
28	Fatboy Slim	Rockafeller Skank
29	Super Furry Animals	Ice Hockey Hair
30	Billy Bragg	Way Over Yonder in the Minor Key
31	Freed Unit	Widishins
32	Male Nurse	My Own Private Patrick Swayze
33	Mercury Rev	Goddess on a Highway
34	Elbow	Powder Blue
35	Gorky's Zygotic Mynci	Sweet Johnny

36	Gorky's Zygotic Mynci	Hush the Warmth
37	Melt Banana	Stimulus for Revolting Virus
38	The Delgados	The Actress
39	Quickspace	If I Were a Carpenter
40	60 Ft Dolls	Alison's Room
41	Boards of Canada	Roig Biv
42	Derero	Radar Intruder
43	Hefner	Pull Yourself Together
44	Roony	Went to Town
45	Sodastream	Turnstile
46	Sportique	The Kids Are Solid Gold
47	Ten Benson	Evil Heat
48	Autechre	Fold Four Rap Five
49	The Fall	Shake Off
50	PJ Harvey	Is This Desire?

1999

1	The Cuban Boys	Cognoscenti vs Intelligentsia
2	Hefner	Hymn for the Cigarettes
3	Hefner	Hymn for the Alcohol
4	The Fall	Touch Sensitive
5	Gorky's Zygotic Mynci	Spanish Dance Troupe
6	Elastica with Mark E Smith	How He Wrote Elastica Man
7	The Fall	F-Oldin' Money
8	The Flaming Lips	Race for the Prize
9	Murry the Hump	Thrown Like a Stone
10	Low	Immune
11	Half Man Half Biscuit	Look Dad No Tunes
12	The Flaming Lips	Superman
13	Cinerama	Pacific
14	Mogwai	Cody
15	Orbital	Style
16	Sonic Subjunkies	Do You Even Know Who You Are?
17	Super Furry Animals	Fire in My Heart

18	Cinerama	King's Cross
19	Salako	Look Left
20	Clinic	The Second Line
21	Godspeed You Black Emperor	Hungover as the Oven At Maida Vale (session)
22	Hefner	I Stole a Bride
23	Bonnie Prince Billy	I See a Darkness
24	Super Furry Animals	Northern Lites
25	Mogwai	Stanley Kubrick
26	Kraken	Side Effects
27	Super Furry Animals	Turning Tide
28	The Cuban Boys	Flossie's Alarming Clock
29	Dawn of the Replicants	Science Fiction Freak
30	Half Man Half Biscuit	24 Hour Garage People (session)
31	Pavement	Major Leagues
32	Hefner	I Took Her Love For Granted
33	Gene	As Good as it Gets
34	Plone	Be Rude to Your School
35	Smog	Cold Blooded Old Times
36	Broadcast	Echoes Answer
37	Add N To X	Metal Finger in My Body
38	Melt Banana	Plot in a Pot
39	Atari Teenage Riot	Revolution Action
40	Blur	Tender
41	Badly Drawn Boy	Once Around the Block
42	Aphex Twin	Windowlicker
43	Six By Seven	Helden
44	Appliance	Food Music
45	Pavement	Carrot Rope
46	Stereolab	The Free Design
47	Marine Research	Parallel Horizontal
48	Miss Mend	Living City Plan
49	Hefner	Hymn For the Things We Didn't Do
50	Wheat	Don't I Hold You
51	Monkey Steals the Drum	Injured Birds

2000

....

1	Neko Case & Her Boyfriends	Twist the Knife
2	PJ Harvey	Good Fortune
3	The Fall	Dr Buck's Letter
4	And You Will Know Us By the Trail of Dead	Mistakes & Regrets
5	Broadcast	Come On Let's Go
6	PJ Harvey	Big Exit
7	Hefner	The Greedy Ugly People
8	Schneider TM	The Light 3000
9	The Delgados	No Danger
10	The Delgados	American Trilogy
11	Low	Dinosaur Act
12	Hefner	The Day That Thatcher Dies
13	Ballboy	I Hate Scotland
14	The Delgados	Accused of Stealing
15	Hefner	Good Fruit
16	Cinerama	Your Charms
17	Cinerama	Wow
18	PJ Harvey	Mess We're In
19	Shellac	Prayer To God
20	Boards of Canada	In a Beautiful Place Out in the Country
21	Laura Cantrell	Somewhere Some Night
22	Calexico	Ballad of Cable Hogue
23	The Fall	Two Librans
24	PJ Harvey	Whore's Hustle, Hustler's Whore
25	Radiohead	Kid A
26	New Order	Brutal
27	Laura Cantrell	Two Seconds
28	Clinic	The Second Line
29	The Cuban Boys	Vinyl Countdown
30	Cowcube	Popping Song
31	Herman Dune	Drug Dealer in the Park
32	Half Man Half Biscuit	24 Hour Garage People

33	Cat Power	Wonderwall (session)
34	Cuban Boys	Theme From Prim & Proper
35	Lab 4	Candyman
36	Gorky's Zygotic Mynci	Fresher Than the Sweetness in Water
37	Half Man Half Biscuit	Irk the Purists
38	The Delgados	Witness
39	Mighty Math	Soul Boy
40	Smog	Dress Sexy at My Funeral
41	Cinerama	Manhattan
42	Laura Cantrell	Queen of the Coast
43	The Fall	WB
44	Hefner	Painting & Kissing
45	Orbital & Angelo Badalamenti	Beached
46	Bonnie Prince Billy	Little Boy Blue
47	Sigur Ros	Svefn G Englar
48	Radiohead	Idiotique
49	Belle & Sebastian	Fought in a War
50	Grandaddy	Crystal Lake

2001

1	Melys	Chinese Whispers
2	The White Stripes	Hotel Yorba
3	Cinerama	Health & Efficiency
4	Bearsuit	Hey Charlie, Hey Chuck
5	The Strokes	Last Night
6	The White Stripes	Fell in Love With a Girl
7	The Strokes	Hard To Explain
8	Camera Obscura	Eighties Fan
9	New Order	Crystal
10	Mogwai	My Father the King
11	Meanwhile, Back in Communist Russia	Morning After Pill
12	Saloon	Impact

13	Half Man Half Biscuit	Bob Wilson Anchorman
14	Miss Black America	Human Punk
15	The Detroit Cobras	Shout Bama Lama
16	Half Man Half Biscuit	Vatican Broadside
17	Belle & Sebastian	Jonathan David
18	The Strokes	The Modern Age
19	Pulp	Sunrise
20	Squarepusher	My Red Hot Car
21	Super Furry Animals	Rings Around the World
22	Mogwai	Two Rights Make One Wrong
23	Cuban Boys	Drink, Drink, Drink
24	Greenskeepers	Low & Sweet
25	The White Stripes	Dead Leaves & the Dirty Ground
26	Ballboy	They'll Hang Flags From Cranes
27	Lift to Experience	These are the Days
28	The Strokes	New York City Cops
29	Pulp	Trees
30	The Fall	I Wake Up in the City
31	Hefner	Alan Bean
32	Belle & Sebastian	I'm Waking Up to Us
33	Ikara Colt	One Note
34	Cinerama	Superman
35	Melys	I Don't Believe in You
36	PJ Harvey	This is Love
37	Seedling	Sensational Vacuum
38	Antihero	Who's Looking Out for Number One
39	Lift to Experience	Falling From Cloud Nine
40	Radiohead	The Pyramid Song
41	Ballboy	I've Got Pictures of You in Your Underwear
42	Miss Black America	Don't Speak My Mind
43	The Shins	New Slang
44	Mercury Rev	Dark is Rising
45	Stereolab	Captain Easychord

46	The Strokes	Someday
47	The Hives	Hate To Say I Told You So
48	The Rock of Travolta	Giant Robo
49	Saloon	Freefall
50	Pico	Chard

2002

1	Saloon	Girls Are the New Boys
2	Cinerama	Quick, Before it Melts
3	Miss Black America	Talk Hard
4	Nina Nastasia	Ugly Face
5	Antihero	Rolling Stones T-Shirt
6	M.A.S.S.	Hey Gravity
7	Laura Cantrell	Too Late For Tonight
8	Pinhole	So Over You
9	Marc Smith vs Safe & Sound	Identify the Beat
10	Ballboy	All the Records on the Radio Are Shite
11	Miss Black America	Miss Black America
12	Yeah Yeah Yeahs	Bang
13	Cinerama	Careless
14	Half Man Half Biscuit	The Light at the End of the Tunnel
15	The White Stripes	Dead Leaves & the Dirty Ground
16	Low	In the Drugs
17	Asa-Chang & Junray	Hana
18	Low	Canada
19	Coin-Op	Democracies
20	Belle & Sebastian	You Send Me (Live At Peel Acres)
21	The Datsuns	In Love
22	The Fall	Susan vs Youthclub
23	Jeffrey Lewis	The Chelsea Hotel Oral Sex Song

24	Ballboy	Where Do the Nights of Sleep Go? (When They Do Not Come To Me)
25	Cornershop	Staging the Plaguing of the Raised Platform
26	Saloon	Have You Seen the Light?
27	The White Stripes	Fell In Love With a Girl
28	The Cranebuilders	Your Song
29	The Delgados	Mr Blue Sky (session)
30	Bearsuit	Drinkink
31	Ladytron	Seventeen
32	Boom Bip & Dose One	Mannequin Trapdoor
33	The Von Bondies	It Came From Japan
34	Wire	99.9 (session)
35	Mclusky	Alan is a Cowboy Killer (That's How You Sing)
36	Low	Amazing Grace
37	Antihero	You Got Nothing (session)
38	Half Man Half Biscuit	Breaking News
39	Cinerama	Cat Girl Tights
40	Mclusky	To Hell With Good Intentions
41	Burning Love Jumpsuit	Cheerleader
42	Interpol	Obstacle 1
43	Melys	So Good
44	The Delgados	Coming in From the Cold
45	Miss Black America	Infinite Chinese Box
46	Eighties Matchbox B-Line Disaster	Celebrate Your Mother
47	The D4	Get Loose
48	Mum	Green Grass of Tunnel
49	Aphrodisiacs	This is a Campaign
50	The Dawn Parade	The Hole in My Heart

2003

1	Cinerama	Don't Touch That Dial

2	The Fall	Theme From Sparta FC
3	Mogwai	Hunted by a Freak
4	The Undertones	Thrill Me
5	Bearsuit	Itsuko Got Married
6	Mogwai	Ratts of the Capital
7	Half Man Half Biscuit	Tending the Wrong Grave For 23 Years
8	The Crimea	Baby Boom
9	C.S.L.M.	John Peel is Not Enough
10	The White Stripes	7 Nation Army
11	Belle & Sebastian	Step Into My Office, Baby
12	Melt Banana	Shield For Your Eyes
13	Nina Nastasia	You, Her & Me
14	Ballboy	The Sash My Father Wore
15	Vive La Fete	Noir Desir
16	Sluts of Trust	Piece O' You
17	The White Stripes	Black Math
18	Yeah Yeah Yeahs	Maps
19	The Broken Family Band	At the Back of the Chapel
20	Darkness Vs S.F.B.	I Believe in a Thing Called Love
21	Million Dead	I Am The Party
22	The Undertones	Oh Please
23	Ballboy	I Gave Up My Eyes
24	Party of One	Shotgun Funeral
25	Futureheads	First Day
26	The Fall	Green Eyed Loco Man
27	French	Porn Shoes
28	Half Man Half Biscuit	It Makes The Room Look Bigger
29	Architecture in Helsinki	The Owls Go
30	Camera Obscura	Suspended From Class
31	Amsterdam	Does This Train Stop on Merseyside?
32	Maher Shalal Hash Baz	Open Field
33	Neulander	Sex, God, Money
34	The Black Keys	Have Love Will Travel

35	M.A.S.S.	Live A Little
36	French	Gabriel in the Airport
37	Radiohead	There, There
38	Ballboy	Born in the USA
39	Cat Power	Werewolf
40	Broadcast	Pendulum
41	The Keys	Strength of Strings
42	Golden Virgins	Renaissance Kids
43	Belle & Sebastian	Stay Loose
44	Hyper Kinako	Tokyo Invention Registration Office
45	Grandmaster Gareth	Dr Dre Buys a Pint of Milk
46	Super Furry Animals	Slow Life
47	Camera Obscura	Keep it Clean
48	Blizzard Boys	Ain't No Stoppin' This
49	Freddy Fresh	You Can See the Paint
50	The Vaults	I'm Going

2004

1	The Fall	Theme from Sparta FC Part 2
2	Bearsuit	Charger
3	Caroline Martin	The Singer
4	Aereogramme	Dreams and Bridges
5	Sluts of Trust	Leave You Wanting More
6	The Delgados	Everybody Come Down
7	Sons & Daughters	Johnny Cash
8	Half Man Half Biscuit	Joy Division
9	Graham Coxon	Freakin' Out
10	Jawbone	Hi De Hi
11	Bloc Party	Helicopter
12	Texas Radio Band	Chwareon
13	Martyn Hare	Do Not Underestimate
14	Cinerama	It's Not You It's Me
15	Aereogramme	The Unravelling
16	P. J. Harvey	The Letter

17	Laura & Ballboy	I Lost You (But I Found Country Music)
18	Jawbone	Jack Rabbit
19	DJ Distance	Ritual
20	Bloc Party	Banquet
21	Ballboy	The Art of Kissing
22	The Black Keys	Ten AM Automatic
23	PJ Harvey	Shame
24	Decoration	It Tried It, I Tried It, I Loved It
25	65 Days of Static	Retreat! Retreat!
26	Mclusky	That Man Will Not Hang
27	Listen With Sarah	Animal Hop
28	XBooty	O Superman
29	Digital Mystikz	B
30	The Black Keys	Girl Is On My Mind
31	Art Brut	Formed A Band
32	The Delgados	I Fought The Angels
33	Shitmat	There's No Business Like Propa' Rungleclotted Mashup Bizznizz
34	The Magic Band	Bug Eyed Beans from Venus
35	Jon E. Cash	International
36	The Wedding Present	Interstate 5
37	Tunng	Tale from Black
38	Melys	Eyeliner
39	Decoration	Joy Adamson
40	Cornershop Presents Bubbley Kaur	Topknot
41	Calvin Party	Northern Song
42	Plasticman	Cha
43	Kentucky AFC	Be Nesa
44	Bloc Party	Little Thoughts
45	Aphrodisiacs	If U Want Me
46	The Mountain Goats	Your Belgian Things
47	The Magic Band	Electricity
48	Ella Guru	Park Lake Speakers
49	Ballboy	I don't have time to stand here

		with you fighting about
		the size of my dick
50	The Vaults	No Sleep No Need

All Time (Millennium)

1	Joy Division	Atmosphere
2	The Undertones	Teenage Kicks
3	Joy Division	Love Will Tear Us Apart
4	The Sex Pistols	Anarchy in the UK
5	The Clash	White Man in Hammersmith Palais
6	New Order	Blue Monday
7	The Smiths	How Soon is Now?
8	Nirvana	Smells Like Teen Spirit
9	The Smiths	There is a Light That Never Goes Out
10	This Mortal Coil	Song to the Siren
11	Robert Wyatt	Shipbuilding
12	Pulp	Common People
13	Captain Beefheart	Big Eyed Beans From Venus
14	Dead Kennedys	Holiday In Cambodia
15	Joy Division	New Dawn Fades
16	My Bloody Valentine	Soon
17	New Order	Ceremony
18	The Only Ones	Another Girl, Another Planet
19	New Order	Temptation
20	Joy Division	She's Lost Control
21	Wedding Present	Brassneck
22	The Smiths	This Charming Man
23	Sugarcubes	Birthday
24	The Fall	How I Wrote 'Elastic' Man
25	Wedding Present	My Favourite Dress
26	The Delgados	Pull the Wires From the Wall
27	My Bloody Valentine	Feed Me With Your Kiss
28	Joy Division	Transmission

29	The Sex Pistols	Pretty Vacant
30	The Pixies	Debaser
31	Belle & Sebastian	Lazy Line Painter Jane
32	New Order	True Faith
33	The Clash	Complete Control
34	The Fall	Totally Wired
35	The Jam	Going Underground
36	Stereolab	French Disco
37	Jimi Hendrix Experience	All Along the Watchtower
38	The Fall	The Classical
39	The Damned	New Rose
40	Tim Buckley	Song to the Siren
41	The Beach Boys	God Only Knows
42	The Velvet Underground	Heroin
43	Nick Drake	Northern Sky
44	Bob Dylan	Visions of Johanna
45	The Beatles	I Am the Walrus
46	The Beach Boys	Good Vibrations
47	The Sundays	Can't Be Sure
48	Culture	Lion Rock
49	PJ Harvey	Shee-La-Na-Gig
50	Pavement	Here

Index

JP refers to John Peel.

Recordings are generally listed under the name of the relevant artist/s. References in *italics* are to albums unless stated otherwise.

For BBC Radio 1 refer to individual programmes and personalities.

Index

Index

funeral 221–4; *see also Home Truths* (BBC Radio 4); individual radio stations and programmes; Peel Acres; Ravenscroft, Shiela

Peebles, Andy 125, 126

Peel Acres (Great Finborough; JP's home) 88, 104, 147, 169, 175, 180, 190, 198

'Peel Sessions, The' (Strange Fruit label) 122

Penetration 107

Perfumed Garden, The (Radio London) 50–1, 53, 54, 56–7, 63, 82, 100, 108

Perkins, Brian 167

Perry, Mark 11

'Pickin the Blues' (Grinderswitch; JP's signature tune) 70, 71, 198, 208

'Pig'(nickname) *see* Ravenscroft, Sheila (JP's wife)

'Pigs Big 78, The' 176

Pink Floyd 4, 51, 65

Pink Pop Festival (Holland) 131

PJ Harvey 1, 176, 214

Plant, Robert 193, 222

Pogues 132

Police 109, 125

Pop, Iggy: 'Lust for Life' 162

Portsmouth University 171

Powell, Anthony: *A Dance to the Music of Time* (novel sequence) 138

Powell, Jonathan 138

Powell, Peter 113, 126

Prescott, John 218–19

Presley, Elvis 31, 39, 106, 227; 'Heartbreak Hotel' 33

Pretenders 133

Principal Edward's Magic Theatre 62

Private Eye (magazine) 30

Prydz, Eric 189

Pulp 22, 120–1, 197, 200

punk rock 10, 53, 63, 95–102, 110, 198–9

Q (magazine) 141

qawwali (music style) 144

Quads 127

Quaker Family in India and Zanzibar, A (ed. Bird; book) 154–5

Queen 4, 129

Quicksilver Messenger Service 63

r&b (music style) 44

Rachmaninov, Sergei: Second Piano Concerto 137

Radcliffe, Mark 22, 142, 171

Radio Academy Hall of Fame 171

Radio Caroline (pirate radio station) 49, 54–5, 221

Radio Eins (Germany) 176